The Ferries of

North Carolina

*Traveling the State's
Nautical
Highways*

Barbara Brannon

WILMINGTON, NORTH CAROLINA
Winoca Press

The Ferries of North Carolina: Traveling the State's Nautical Highways
© 2007 Barbara Brannon

Except where noted, photographs are by the author. Other photos used by permission. State ferry schedules courtesy of Ferry Division, North Carolina Department of Transportation; updated schedules may be found at www.ncdot.org/transit/ferry.

On the cover: M/V *Neuse* in port at Cherry Branch, 2004

This book was set in the Bell Gothic, Adobe Caslon, and Hattenschweiler fonts and printed in the United States of America.
10 09 08 07
10 9 8 7 6 5 4 3 2 1 e

Published by Winoca Press
P. O. Box 30
Wilmington NC 28402-0030
www.winocapress.com

Library of Congress Cataloging-in-Publication Data

Brannon, Barbara.
    The ferries of North Carolina : traveling the state's nautical highways /
Barbara A. Brannon. — 1st North American ed.
        p. cm.
    Includes bibliographical references and index.
    ISBN-13: 978-0-9755910-2-4
    ISBN-10: 0-9755910-2-9
    1. Ferries—North Carolina. I. Title.
    HE5783.N8B73 2006
    386′.609756—dc22
                                                        2006030311

www.ferriesofnorthcarolina.com

ferrytales@ferriesofnorthcarolina.com

"Ferry me across the water,
Do, boatman, do."
"If you've a penny in your purse
I'll ferry you."

CHRISTINA GEORGINA ROSSETTI

Flood-tide below me! I see you face to face!
Clouds of the west—sun there half an hour high—I see you also face to face.

Crowds of men and women attired in the usual costumes, how curious
    you are to me!
On the ferry-boats the hundreds and hundreds that cross, returning home,
    are more curious to me than you suppose,
And you that shall cross from shore to shore years hence are more to me,
    and more in my meditations, than you might suppose.

WALT WHITMAN, "Crossing Brooklyn Ferry"

We were very tired, we were very merry—
We had gone back and forth all night on the ferry.

EDNA ST. VINCENT MILLAY, "Recuerdo"

The Ferries of North Carolina

Route numbers correspond to chapters; detailed maps accompany each chapter

Maps © 2006 Barbara A. Brannon

Contents & maps

Acknowledgments · · · · · · vi

How to Use This Book · · · · · · vii

Introduction
The lure and lore of ferries · · · · · · 1

PART I Traversing Waterways through Time
A brief history of ferries in North Carolina · · · · · · 3

PART II From Port to Passage
How ferries operate · · · · · · 15

PART III The Ferry Experience
Helpful hints for travelers · · · · · · 23

PART IV The North Carolina State Ferry System · · · · · · 31
1 Southport–Fort Fisher · · · · · · 37 46
2 Cherry Branch–Minnesott Beach · · · · · · 49 54
3 Aurora–Bayview · · · · · · 57 62
4 Cedar Island–Ocracoke · · · · · · 65 72
5 Swan Quarter–Ocracoke · · · · · · 75 80
6 Ocracoke–Hatteras · · · · · · 83 92
7 Currituck–Knotts Island · · · · · · 95 100

PART V Other Ferries Serving North Carolina's Islands · · · · · · 103
8 Bald Head Island · · · · · · 107 116
9 Wilmington / Eagles Island · · · · · · 119 116
10 Hammocks Beach State Park / Bear Island · · · · · · 125 122
11 Cape Lookout National Seashore / Shackleford Banks · · · · · · 131 123
12 Cape Lookout National Seashore / South Core Banks · · · · · · 141 123
13 Cape Lookout National Seashore / North Core Banks · · · · · · 151 123
14 Cape Lookout National Seashore / Portsmouth Island · · · · · · 157 123

PART VI The Last of the State's River Ferries · · · · · · 163
15 Elwell Ferry, Cape Fear River · · · · · · 165 170
16 Sans Souci, Cashie River · · · · · · 173 178
17 Parker's Ferry, Meherrin River · · · · · · 181 178

PART VII Further Reading on Ferries · · · · · · 187

PART VIII Sources Used in This Book · · · · · · 191

Acknowledgments

THIS BOOK COVERS FERRIES operated by the state of North Carolina as well as privately operated ferries within the state. Safety and inspection of all ferries in the state is governed by the United States Coast Guard and the North Carolina State Department of Transportation, Ferry Division.

For their assistance with every aspect of this book, thanks go to the dedicated staff, present and former, of the North Carolina Ferry Division, and the dozens of ferry crew and staff whom I interviewed. I would also like to thank the Ferry Division staff for allowing me to draw extensively from their unpublished account of the state ferry system. I greatly appreciate the contributions of the many ferry crew and passengers, anonymous and named, who shared their stories and impressions with me. The Ferry Division was extremely generous in giving me access to information, photographs, and the boats and crews themselves. In times of heightened national security, I realize such access does not come easily, and I appreciate their trust as I pursued this project.

All photographs are my original work unless noted otherwise. Historical photos are used with permission of the copyright holders. Many historical photos were provided by the North Carolina State Archives and the North Carolina Room, New Hanover County Public Library. Maps were designed by Donna Ratzel.

I would like to thank Mary Smith (Britt Services, Inc.) and Eldridge Baker (Baker Services), employees of the private contractors for North Carolina's river ferries, as well as the Russ family of Kelly, N.C., for their assistance. I also want to thank Christi Golder and Jennifer Wilson-Mathis, and the ferry crews of Bald Head Island, Ltd., for arranging informative trips to the island and providing background information. Bo Anderson, Josh Arthur, Rudy Austin, Caroline Corwin, Mike Cruise, Paul Donnelly, Karen Duggan, Ronald Fisher, June Fulcher, Rose Hatcher, John Loonam, Chuck Marriner, Kari Martin, Annette and Art Noyes, Annette Willis Mitchum, and Rob Passfield contributed greatly to my understanding of coastal waters and ferrying.

Thanks go to Bob Pittman of Greenville, N.C., who shared his recollections of the ferries and first told me about Parker's Ferry; to Lucia Peel Powe of Williamston, whose novel features a Francis Speight painting of the Sans Souci Ferry on the cover; to Geraldine Hewett for information on Bald Head Island and Southport; and to Carolyn Rawls Booth and Dick Booth of Cary and Cindy Horrell Ramsey of Atkinson, who shared information about the Elwell Ferry. Bill Morris read the text in an earlier form and offered timely and informed insights.

As always, I acknowledge the assistance and encouragement of my writing and publishing colleagues at the University of North Carolina Wilmington and former colleagues at the University of South Carolina.

I owe a special debt of thanks and fond memories to my late grandparents, who first took me to *roide* (as they would have said) the ferry.

And last, thanks to Kay, fellow traveler on the ferries.

BARBARA BRANNON

How to use this book

NORTH CAROLINA IS A GEOGRAPHICALLY DIVERSE STATE whose boundaries encompass some 3,570 square miles of inland waters, eighteen major rivers, and scores of islands large and small. Its ocean coastline stretches for 301 miles; its total shoreline measures more than 3,000 miles. Many of its watercourses form wide divides between isolated places not readily bridged.

North Carolina has the **second largest system of vehicle and passenger ferries in the nation**, after Washington State. Tourists, commuters, schoolchildren, commercial vehicles, and the military all make use of the state's ferries. The state system maintains an unparalleled safety record, and the network of public and private ferries provides a convenient and enjoyable way to traverse many of the state's complex waterways. All of the ferries still operating in North Carolina are located on or near the coast, in that region that lies to the east of I-95.

The people who keep the ferries running—in administrative offices, in shipyards, on shore, or on the boats—are an amazing group. Although many of them have served on the ferries for a very long time, inevitably there is change in personnel, so this guide does not attempt to list them. Nonetheless, they are vital: **the North Carolina Ferry Division alone employs some 400 men and women.** It's difficult to calculate the direct and indirect effects the ferries have on the state's commerce and tourism.

Detailed driving directions are provided in each section of this book. When you use them, make sure to allow plenty of travel time, as approach roads are often isolated and narrow, with lowered speed limits and numerous turns off the main route. The state's blue directional signs are handily posted, but they're easy to miss when drivers are enjoying the scenery or, in bad weather, dealing with unfamiliar directions and darkness.

If you are traveling to coastal North Carolina from outside the state—or by means other than car—the Insider's Guides, in print and online at www.insiders.com, provide marvelously detailed information about access by highway, water, or air. You'll also find copious and up-to-date listings for lodging, dining, and recreation there, as this volume is not intended to serve as a comprehensive tourism guide.

A word about schedules. The state ferries generally run on time and dependably, from dawn until in many cases well after dark, seven days a week. (None of the ferries operates 24 hours a day or makes overnight runs, as is the case in some parts of the world.) Schedules vary considerably between high season (April through November) and off-season, and at peak times on some routes reservations are not only advisable but necessary. Weather conditions, such as high winds and hurricanes, or flooded approach roadways, may delay or cancel scheduled runs.

The three cable ferries operate on demand during posted hours (again, high-season and off-season hours apply); if water or weather conditions prevent crossings, signs and barriers are generally posted on approach roads to warn travelers.

Private ferries to North Carolina's boat-access-only islands operate seasonally as well, so it is vital to verify schedules and make reservations in the early stages of planning a trip.

Information and schedules provided in this book are current as of fall 2006 but are **subject to change.**

Everyone who rides the ferries has a story—and I invite readers to visit the website for this book and share their own "ferry tales" at **www.ferriesofnorthcarolina.com.** You are welcome to post accounts and photos from your own travels, as the journey continues.

The *Pamlico* in port at the Cedar Island terminal

The lure and lore of
ferries

UNLIKE TALL SHIPS with their breathtaking array of white sails, or ocean liners with their proud bow and sleek layers of decks, ferryboats can seem rather ordinary. With shallow drafts that enable them to navigate inland waters, a wide beam to carry vehicle loads, and an often unimposing superstructure, ferries aren't usually considered the beauty queens of the nautical world. So why is it we find them so intriguing? What is it we love about riding the ferry?

Just as railroad travel represents, for most folks, a romantic and scenic departure from the everyday automobile, the ferry harks back to an earlier, gentler era when travelers were carried and chauffeuered and catered to. The ferry provides an opportunity to enjoy wide-open vistas, to skim across the water while leaving the driving in the hands of a capable crew. It offers a rare—and inexpensive—chance to experience something of what the privileged class of a bygone age might have been accustomed to.

On an afternoon crossing from Southport to Fort Fisher a few years ago, those of us leaning at the ferry rail to watch the waves and the birds were greeted with an unusual sight: an enormous cruise ship that appeared on the horizon to our stern and in short order passed us heading up the Cape Fear River to the port at Wilmington. As the gleaming white liner towered over us momentarily and we looked up with awe at its shapely decks, colorful pennants, and angled smokestacks, the ferry captain's voice came over the loudspeaker: "She's a lot bigger than we are, ladies and gentlemen, but it costs a heck of a lot more'n three dollars to ride her." (The auto fare on the route is five dollars these days.)

"SHE'S A LOT BIGGER THAN WE ARE, LADIES AND GENTLEMEN, BUT IT COSTS A HECK OF A LOT MORE THAN THREE DOLLARS TO RIDE HER."

We chuckled and waved at the well-heeled passengers looming above, watched the ship steam off upriver, and congratulated ourselves on our bargain cruise. For many riders, ferries represent a special treat, an occasional trip to an island vacation destination or a short sightseeing diversion. But ferries also carry passengers (with or without their vehicles) on daily

North Carolina's unspoiled barrier-island beaches are most easily reached by ferry.

commutes to work and school. They transport mail and supplies to remote communities. They shuttle trucks hauling fuel, building materials, and freight. When Hurricane Isabel wrecked roads and houses on North Carolina's Outer Banks in 2003, an additional ferry route was added temporarily from Stumpy Point to Hatteras, carrying heavy loads of lumber, stone, and asphalt to the distant island, then returning to the mainland with storm debris for disposal. Ferry personnel offered their services selflessly to the stranded communities until regular transportation could be restored.

Ferries go back for millennia in our culture and history—recall Charon of Greek mythology, who carried souls across the river of the underworld. In the early years of exploration and settlement in North America, ferries served as vital route across the great continent's network of rivers, until bridges could be constructed, or in places where bridges were not physically or economically feasible. In many communities throughout the nation today, ferries remain the only viable link between mainland and remote islands or peninsulas; in others, ferries provide a quieter, less stressful alternative to highway travel.

If you're reading this aboard one of North Carolina's dozens of ferryboats, I hope you'll enjoy the stories and take away some interesting information. But don't neglect to look out the window or over the rail and appreciate the scenery, and don't miss the opportunity to talk with fellow passengers or helpful crew. And if you're reading this in the landlocked security of home, library, or bookstore—well, what are you waiting for?

Get to the ferry and go for a ride!

traversing waterways through time: a brief history of ferries in north carolina

NORTH CAROLINA'S VAST NETWORK of waterways spreads like a fan from the Piedmont foothills across the coastal plain. There, a dozen rivers empty into broad sounds and bays separated from the Atlantic Ocean by a chain of isolated barrier islands. Early explorers and colonists found it far easier to travel by water than by land, as settlements were separated by dense forests and impenetrable swamps. But as they began to cut roads and tracks through the wilderness, often following paths established by natives or marching armies, they needed a way to carry people and goods across rivers and streams. Long before the automobile, the airplane, or even the railroad, ferries were often the only way to traverse these myriad bodies of water.

Before highways and bridges

Ferries operated at scores of North Carolina river crossings from the eighteenth century through the end of the nineteenth, when bridges and improved roads began to outpace them.

Flat-bottomed wooden boats guided by a rope stretched across the water were used for river crossings. Passengers on foot, buggies and wagons drawn by draft animals, and livestock and cargoes could all make the crossing on the low platform flanked by rails and equipped with loading ramps at either end.

In the nineteenth century, ferries were little more than rafts poled or rowed across the river. The magazine illustration above shows the Cape Fear River ferry at Wilmington in the late 1800s. (Courtesy North Carolina State Archives)

In many communities, farmers used the ferries to transport crops to market, doctors

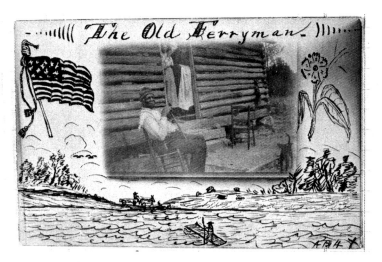

Huss, the "old ferryman" who piloted the platform ferry across the Cape Fear River at Averasboro, c. 1890. (From Albert B. Harrell, "Early Days in Dunn," Harnett County Library; courtesy North Carolina State Archives)

doned. Most riverfront towns have a road or two with "Ferry" in the name (like Old Ferry Road, just off Sabbath Home Road, NC 130, in south Brunswick County, which used to provide access to Holden Beach across the Intracoastal Waterway). Ferry Point is located across the Perquimans River from Hertford in Bertie County; New Ferry Road leads from Gatesville through the Chowan Swamp down to the Chowan River. There's a Cannon Ferry Road near NC 32 in Chowan County. And at Harrellsville, Old Ferry Road signals the place where the ferry used to cross the Wiccacon River, a small tributary of the Chowan.

used them to make house calls, and itinerant preachers used them to travel the circuit. Bishop Francis Asbury, the famous Methodist minister, noted in his journal of May 1800 a ferry crossing in the state's western mountains: "North Carolina, Saturday 8. We started away. The cold was severe upon the fingers. We crossed the ferry, curiously contrived with a rope and pole, for half a mile along the banks of the river, to guide the boat by. The ferrykeeper pulled the rope to haul the boat by hand or used a pole to provide propulsion, while the rope ensured that the boat did not stray with the current." Then as now, flood conditions could prevent the ferry from running.

Today, place names across the state provide a clue to locations long ago aban-

Ferries on North Carolina's rivers

The Moseley map of 1733 indicates numerous ferries named for landowners or operators, among them Bell, Cheshire, Graves, Newby, Sawyer, Simmons, and White. In former times, Blossom's Ferry was an important crossing on the Cape Fear River just north of Wilmington. Sneads Ferry, which once operated across the New River Inlet, now lends its name to the fishing village in Onslow County. Hall's Ferry crossed the Yadkin between Davie and Forsyth Counties, and several different ferries operated on the Pee Dee River between Rockingham and Little River, S.C. Street's Ferry, on the Neuse River near New Bern in Craven County, operated until 1960 at a site that had been served by a ferry since the days of George Washington; Eaton's Ferry operated on the Roanoke River in Warren County until 1961.

By the first decade of the twentieth century, when gasoline-powered automobiles began to appear even in the state's rural counties, enterprising ferry operators had also learned to rig the old rope-drawn ferries with engines, and steel cables began to replace ropes across the rivers.

Despite its efforts to earn the nickname "The Good Roads State" in the 1920s, North Carolina was slow to make substantial progress in highway improvements, so many ferries continued to operate well into the twentieth century (the port city of Wilmington, for instance—the state's largest city until the 1900s—had no highway bridge across the Cape Fear River until 1926 and was served by a ferry docking at the foot of Market Street as late as the 1940s). A 1921 legislative act provided for a state highway system to link all the state's county seats by the most direct route—though ferry service to connect the last few was nearly twenty more years in coming.

In 1960, the state still had five cable-drawn ferries working its rivers; by the 1970s the number had dwindled to the three that continue today. In the era of superhighways, the river ferries are more of a curiosity and tourist draw than essential link, though they do cut miles off the land route in areas where no bridges exist.

Above: Flat-bottomed wooden boats, like this one on the Pee Dee River about 1910, served to carry wagons—and later, automobiles—across many of the state's rivers. (Courtesy North Carolina State Archives)

Below: By the twentieth century, motorized vessels could carry numerous vehicles and passengers in comfort. The steamer ferry *John Knox* plies the Cape Fear River at Wilmington, ca. 1920s. (Courtesy Robert M. Fales Collection, New Hanover County Public Library)

There is something primitive in riding the small inland ferries, not much different from the ways of earlier centuries—a satisfying link with the past even when a ten-mile drive out of the way doesn't amount to much of an inconvenience. It removes the driver from control of the vehicle for a few brief moments and allows riders to be carried, that most elemental of desires. As for the people who operate the vessels—they have to be content with a slower pace of life, blessed with patience, able to find satisfaction in the remote woods, deep waters, wildlife, and forest.

Coastal ferries

The coastal ferries face a different set of challenges. They must operate in very shallow bodies of water that are susceptible to ever-changing currents, winds, and tides. Crossing times are relatively longer, and the vessels must be capable of managing and carrying many more vehicles and passengers. The links they provide between widely separated islands are indispensable, as they are the only regular means of connection for several of the island communities.

In the early days, ferry service was provided by families who knew and understood the coastal climate and waters and who had been engaged in fisheries or boatbuilding. These days, their descendants are likely also to operate guide services and tourist accommodations in addition to the ferries.

Origins of a modern ferry system

Coastal ferries were first established from the mainland to the Outer Banks by private entrepreneurs with tugs and wooden barges. Jack Nelson and, later, Captain J. B. (Toby) Tillett began crossing Oregon Inlet between

Ferry to Hatteras from Engelhard, on the Dare County peninsula, May 1948. The boat that took passengers and their station wagons to the Outer Banks seems also to have had the job of returning hundreds of soda-pop bottles from the island for deposit. (Courtesy North Carolina State Archives)

Hatteras Island and Nags Head in the mid-1920s (before there were even any roads to the southern end of Hatteras Island). Farther north, in the early 1940s T. A. Baum of Kitty Hawk instituted service across Croatan Sound from Manns Harbor to Roanoke Island, using two ten-car-capacity wooden ferryboats called *Tyrrell* and *Dare*.

In North Carolina, development of a statewide highway system also called for the development of ferries and bridges, and by 1934 the state highway commission began subsidizing private ferry routes to make tolls affordable to travelers. In 1938 the state promised to increase its subsidy to offset tolls completely. From 1942 to 1961 the service was fully subsidized and remained free to travelers.

The "North Carolina Navy"

In 1947, the North Carolina Highway Commission bought its first ferry service outright. From Baum's widow, the agency acquired the Croatan Sound route from Manns Harbor to Manteo, and so was born the "North Carolina Navy"—a fond nickname for the

Above: Early wooden ferries such as the original *Tyrrell* and *Dare* carried vehicles to the Outer Banks—but island roads were merely tracks in the sand until the 1950s. (Courtesy North Carolina State Archives)

Below: The *Governor Scott*, a modified military craft, replaced its wooden counterpart on the Alligator River ferry route in 1950. (Courtesy North Carolina State Archives)

state ferry system. That same year, the state also began to operate a ferry across the Alligator River between Tyrrell and Dare Counties. The state acquired Tillett's Oregon Inlet route in 1950.

The vessels the government purchased to serve these routes were initially the same wooden boats that had been in private use for years. In the decade after World War II, the ferry service converted military landing craft—steel-hulled LCTs (Landing Craft, Tank) designed for transporting troops and artillery to beaches—into car ferries. Each of these converted boats had a capacity of twenty-one cars. The vessels were named *Governor Cherry* in honor of then governor Gregg Cherry and *Sandy Graham* in honor of the State Highway Commission chairman. The old *Tyrrell* and *Dare* were decommissioned and sold. Another converted LCT, the *Governor Scott*, was put into service.

Though sturdy and reliable, the LCTs had never been intended for long-term use, and their hulls frequently required repair after scraping the shallow bottoms of the sound. In addition, vehicle traffic was rising steadily following the paving of NC Highway 12 on the Outer Banks and the establishment of the Cape Hatteras National Seashore in 1953, and greater

Outer Banks visitors awaiting the ferry *Sea Level,* early 1960s. (Courtesy North Carolina State Archives)

By the time the Chesapeake Bay Bridge and Tunnel system in Virginia was opened in 1954, more Northern tourists than ever began venturing down to the Outer Banks. The Governor Umstead Bridge, completed over Croatan Sound in December 1956, opened the islands to easy access from North Carolina's mainland cities. Outer Banks ferries continued to carry traffic, for free, across the Alligator River between Sandy Point and East Lake until 1961, across Oregon Inlet between Nags Head and Hatteras until 1962, and across Hatteras Inlet beginning in 1957 and continuing today.

Just as bridges put older routes and vessels out of commission, however, new routes were introduced in the 1960s. The expansion of the system required tolls on several routes to offset maintenance and operation costs.

In 1960 the Taylor brothers, shipping contractors and hotel operators from Atlantic, N.C., built a 128-foot ferry, the *Sea Level,* to begin a Pamlico Sound crossing between Atlantic and Ocracoke Island, providing the only car access to the southern end of the Outer Banks. Within the year the Taylors sought to sell their operation to the state, which eventually voted to acquire it and in 1961 made the run its first toll route. The one-way fare ranged from $6.75 for car and driver up to $22.25 for the longest trailers and $35.25 for tractor-trailers; the ferry made one round trip daily.

Ferryboats were soon put into service on Bogue Sound bewteen Cape Carteret and Emerald Isle as well. The additional ferry

carrying capacity was called for. The state later began constructing new boats in a "double-ended" style (that is, which could be driven from either end, avoiding the need for turning to unload) specifically designed for the Outer Banks ferry routes. By the 1960s North Carolina had built a fleet of state-of-the-art ferryboats, and all of the old LCTs were retired by the 1970s.

Transportation and tourism

Ferry routes were initially established to serve local enterprise and government: their purpose was to provide access for farmers and loggers to bring their goods to market, and to give citizens of distant regions easier access to county seats. But it became apparent that tourism was a major incentive as well. The surge in leisure travel after the end of World War II brought automobiles to North Carolina's remote coasts in growing numbers.

crossings were instantly popular with vaca-tioners, who seemed to take tolls and long summer lines in stride.

In the fall of 1962, the state estab-lished a ferry specifically designed to transport school children across Currituck Sound between Knotts Island and Cur-rituck, halving the time required for a 90-minute bus ride into Virginia and back down to the mainland. A six-car ferry, christened M/V *Knotts Island*, was con-structed for the purpose.

Expansion of the state ferry system

Other major changes to the ferry service occurred in the 1960s. On the Outer Banks, the construction of the tall Herbert C. Bonner Bridge brought forty years of ferry operation across Oregon Inlet to an end in 1963.

The following year, the Pamlico Sound service was shifted from Atlantic to a deeper-water route departing from Cedar Island, reducing the four-hour crossing time to less than three hours so that a second daily run could be added. That same year, the headquarters for the ferry system was moved from Manteo to Morehead City, to better support the service's planned expan-sion southward.

For decades citizens had petitioned for a ferry route crossing the Cape Fear River between Southport and Fort Fisher. A bill approving the route was finally approved by the state legislature in 1964, and the new route was inaugurated on Tuesday, February 8, 1966. Newspapers reported that the new route was "an instant success" that would soon provide ready access to the beaches of

Brunwsick County. The workhorse ferryboat *Sea Level*, which had formerly made the run from Cedar Island to Ocracoke, was placed in service on the new route.

In March 1966, a sixth state ferry operation was initiated, spanning the Pam-lico River from Gaylord's Bay, near Bayview

Dignitaries aboard the M/V *Sea Level* at the inaguration of a route across the Cape Fear River between Southport and Fort Fisher, Feb. 8, 1966. (Courtesy North Carolina State Archives)

in Beaufort County, to Huddles Cut, near Aurora, primarily to provide transportation for employees of a newly opened phosphate mining operation.

By 1967 riders were clamoring for reduction or removal of tolls, which were considered too steep, or detrimental to economic development. They realized a moderate success in their endeavor, and fares have remained afforable ever since.

In 1972 the Bogue Sound ferry operation was discontinued when the Cameron B. Langston Bridge was opened. At that time the route had been the state's busiest, with more than a quarter million vehicles transported in its final year. One of the boats from the closed operation was refitted and reassigned to a new route on the Neuse River between Minnesott Beach in Pamlico County and Cherry Branch in Craven County, primarily serving commuters to the Cherry Point Marine Air Base.

A seventh state ferry operation was formed in 1977. The Swan Quarter/Ocracoke crossing was instituted across Pamlico Sound

The M/V *Cedar Island,* like all of the vessels in North Carolina's state ferry fleet, is registered out of Morehead City, where the Ferry Division's headquarters is located.

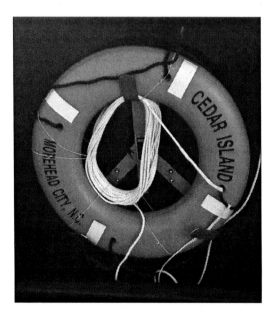

to link Ocracoke residents with their county seat on the mainland. The M/V *Governor Edward Hyde,* a thirty-car-capacity ferry, was built for the crossing and remains in service there today.

The Ferry Division is born

The entire state ferry operation underwent reorganization after a 1970s study, and the Ferry Division of the State Highway Department was officially created on July 1, 1974. In the 1970s, the state also took over responsibility for the three remaining river ferries, contracting out their operation to a private firm.

During the 1980s, the Ferry Division initiated an ambitious program of upgrading its equipment and extending carrying capacity. Hulls were lengthened on some of the boats, and larger or more efficient vessels were constructed for other routes. Many of the new vessels were funded through the Federal Highway Administration's (FHWA) Intermodal Surface Transportation Efficiency Act (ISTEA) program of the 1990s, which was reauthorized in 1999 as the Transportation Efficiency Act. The program helped increase the number of departures and reduce waiting times.

The first boat to be built under the FHWA ISTEA program, in 1992, was the M/V *Governor Daniel Russell* on the Southport–Fort Fisher route. It was also the first double-ended ferry in the North Carolina fleet; for the first time, vehicles could load on the bow and exit off the stern and vice versa, eliminating the need for the vessel to turn around on each run. The system's newer ferries are driven by a safe and efficient Voith-

The M/V *Southport* is decked out in the blue and white of Duke University.

Schneider propulsion system, which works without propellers and rudders to deliver power and steering in shallow waters.

Education and environment

In 1994 the Ferry Division introduced an imaginative plan to honor education in the state and to brighten the ferry paint schemes. Ferry Division director Jerry Gaskill gained approval from the board of governors of the University of North Carolina system to trim the ferries in the school colors of the sixteen state-supported institutions of higher education. The program was such a succcess that it was later expanded to include the largest private universities and colleges in the

Right: Schoolchildren taking the ferry between Knotts Island and Currituck, 2002. Junior high and high school students still travel to school on the mainland via ferry. (Courtesy North Carolina Ferry Division)

state. (See pages 32–35 for the institutions honored on each route.)

The ferries' impact in the 21st century

Over the years, ferries have played a major role in the development of the state, as they do even today. Many of the most heavily traveled bridges in North Carolina span routes that were originally linked by ferry. Dozens of coastal communities have depended on ferry service as their main contact with the outside world, for daily necessities such as food, medicine, and mail. Schoolchildren are transported from remote towns to schools on the mainland, and citizens with business to conduct in county-seat towns on the mainland are able to do so more conveniently with ferries to transport them there.

Since its inception, the North Carolina Ferry Division has also played a major role in the evacuation of residents and visitors from the Outer Banks during the periods of hurricanes and other disasters. At such times

the Ferry Division often provides the sole source of relief to outlying areas.

Currently the North Carolina Ferry Division is the second largest system in the United States, second in route miles to the Washington State system. The North Carolina Ferry System transports more than 1.2 million vehicles and 2.5 million passengers annually across seven routes throughout the eastern part of the state. The twenty-four vessels in the North Carolina ferry fleet are some of the safest and most dependable in the world.

Not only do the ferries transport much-needed goods and services to isolated areas of the state—they also provide an impor-

tant source of employment in areas where jobs are relatively scarce. Working for the ferries is a time-honored tradition in many coastal communities, helping to preserve a strong local heritage and a unique livelihood from the Outer Banks to Down East to the coastal rivers.

The state ferry system also assists in water quality research and monitoring in the Albemarle-Pamlico Estuarine System. The FerryMon program was introduced on three state-owned ferries beginning in 2000, with the assistance of the Institute of Marine Sciences and UNC– Chapel Hill, the Duke University Marine

Laboratory, the North Carolina Department of Envrionment and Natural Resources, and the Carolina Envrionmental Program at UNC–Chapel Hill. The project's aim is to study water quality in North America's second largest estuary and its impact on fish habitats in the region. FerryMon has become a model nationwide for such studies.

Each participating ferry houses a flow-through system for sampling of near surface water, which is automatically tested for such factors as surface water temperature, salinity, dissolved oxygen, pH level, turbidity, and fluorescence of chlorophyll. The sample data are matched up to precise time and location by an onboard computer and then downloaded nightly to a computer located at the Duke University Marine Laboratory in Beaufort.

This unique partnership provides a long-term, cost-effective monitoring system to evaluate environmental status and trends—issues of concern far beyond the state's own borders and waters.

Tourism and recreation, which grew so rapidly in the years following World War II, continue to be a chief reason for the ferries' vigorous presence in North Carolina. In 2004 the North Carolina Travel Industry Association recognized the Ferry Division with its Bill Sharpe Travel Award, an annual honor given to individuals and/or organizations that have contributed selflessly to the travel industry of North Carolina. The Ferry Division was the first government agency to receive the award.

A series of beautifully photographed ads in North Carolina's *Our State* magazine captures the allure of the ferries as a route to adventure, to scenic beauty, to rest and relaxation, and to time away from the ordinary world.

The ferries may have changed dramatically in operation, in purpose, and in location over the years. But their appeal as a way to escape the cares and pace of the mainland remains unrivaled.

A crewman on the M/V *Southport* lowers the off-ramp to the deck of the boat.

from **port** to **passage**
how **ferries** operate

A FERRY, ACCORDING TO ONE definition, is a "ship carrying passengers and or vehicles engaged in regular short voyages, e.g., across a river or narrow body of water, between two or more places or ports" (www.deck-officer.com/glossary). The primary issues for ferries—as with all marine vessels—are how to make the boat float reliably, how to make the boat go efficiently, and how to carry passengers and payload safely.

Today's car and passenger ferries have come a long way since the towboat-and-barge operations of earlier decades. The North Carolina state ferry system maintains a fleet designed specifically for the state's broad, shallow waters, and it holds an excellent safety record. The privately operated river ferries are also fully mechanized and remarkably efficient, carrying a vehicle across in less than ten minutes from load to unload.

All North Carolina passenger and vehicle ferries are built and maintained in accordance with the relevant portion of the U.S. Code of Federal Regulation (CFR). Crew training and licensing, certification for seaworthiness, and inspection are handled by the U.S. Coast Guard. In addition, the North Carolina Ferry Division is a member of the Passenger Vessel Association, the trade organization for the industry in North America.

A few facts and figures

North Carolina's coastal ferries must be able to operate in shallow water depth—vessels are required to run at a minimum loaded draft of 5' to 6.5' (barely over the head of an average person!). For this reason they are limited in size, carrying 20 to 25 vehicles (40 to 42 vehicles for the River Class boats), and must maintain a frequent schedule, staffed by highly trained and specialized crew, to handle demand.

While ferryboats in many locations in the world are more like ocean liners, North Carolina's largest ferries are only 220 feet in length. The designation M/V (Motor Vessel) is used for all the state's coastal ferryboats. The vessels currently in North Carolina's fleet were specially designed for the purpose. Though a couple were built in local shipyards, most were built in yards based on the Gulf of Mexico, including several new double-ended boats placed in service in 2003 and 2006.

Propulsion and navigation

North Carolina's shallow-draft boats carry vehicles on a single flat metal deck above the water line, with additional upper decks for passenger areas, the bridge, and navigation and instrumentation. Heavy steel-paneled rails surround the vehicle deck, except at the bow and stern where vehicles load and unload. Two poles are positioned to help the captain line up the boat for docking; during landing, they keep the box and stern lined up so that the car ramp will be properly oriented on the vessel's centerline.

Below the vehicle deck is located the engine room, where the mechanisms that provide power and steering operate below the water line. North Carolina's large (180' and 220') ferryboats travel at an average speed of 12 knots (imagine a car going about 14 miles per hour); smaller vessels run at 10 knots.

Two ways to move

The North Carolina Ferry Division's boats feature several different configurations. On single-ended boats, such as the M/V *Carteret* and the M/V *Cape Point,* the propulsion is provided at the stern. The vessel loads from bow or stern, and it must turn around in the harbor before docking to unload vehicles and load again. Single-ended vessels use conventional twin-screw propulsion, with a pair of propellers aft (at the stern) driven by a diesel-fueled propulsion engine through a line shaft. Steering on conventional-propulsion vessels is accomplished by an electric-over-hydraulic-system that moves the rudders in response to the wheel.

Double-ended vessels eliminate the need for turning to discharge vehicles. These vessels are symmetrical, with propulsion provided at both ends (note the "A" and "B" marked on the rails of these boats—the bow becomes the stern, and the stern becomes the

The Voith-Schneider propulsion system, designed in Germany, operates like an underwater helicopter blade to move a ferryboat in shallow water. (Diagram courtesy of NC Ferry Division)

The engine room of the M/V *Southport,* North Carolina's first ferry to feature the cycloidal Voith-Schneider propulsion system

Working with wind and water

The situation of broad, shallow water is compounded in North Carolina by wind-driven tides that are not always as predictable as lunar tides. If a nor'easter comes up—a storm that brings heavy rain and wind out of the north rather than from the tropics—the wind can actually "blow out" parts of a body of water, creating impassable shallows.

bow). Some of these boats use conventional screw propellers at each end.

The newest vessels in the state ferry fleet employ the advanced Voith-Schneider cycloidal propulsion system, a German design that works without propellers and rudders. Functioning a bit like a helicopter blade, this system propels the vessel by changing the pitch of a series of fins rotating at a constant RPM to provide both the thrust (the greater the angle of pitch, the faster the boat moves) and the steering. The Voith-Schneider system delivers remarkable maneuverability, using a thrust-orienting propeller in each end of the vessel to direct power in any direction. Vessels equipped with it can go forward, aft, sideways, or crab, or rotate 360 degrees while not moving in any direction.

Conversely, there's little danger of a ferry capsizing in such waters. The Ferry Division has never had a major incident, in which a boat has sunk. All of the state-owned vessels have radar and a gyroscopic or magnetic compass. The majority are also equipped with GPS (Global Positioning System). Four of the Sound Class vessels have "auto-pilot" capabilities. Highly skilled captains—licensed only after many years of successively demanding training and on-the-job experience—bring their knowledge of wind, water, and weather to bear on each day's unique challenges. And, like all commercial vessels, they monitor radio channel 16, the Coast Guard emergency and hailing channel, from the bridge.

To learn more about the geometry (buoyancy, displacement, heel, trim, stability,

A morning aboard the *Gov. Edward Hyde*

On the long Swan Quarter–to–Ocracoke route, mate W. G. Mason, a wiry, sixty-something-looking fellow with a glint of humor in his eye, takes a moment to talk to me about the boat's operation. Who are the passengers, mainly? In the summer, mostly tourists, he says. But in the winter it's largely locals who have business on the mainland. Commuters who work at the phosphate plant in Aurora, for instance, or at the air base. Hyde Countians from Ocracoke must travel in to Swan Quarter to take care of legal and civic affairs, one of the primary reasons for this ferry route's existence.

Mason takes me up to the bridge to speak with Capt. L. M. Mason—no relation—who, after phoning in to headquarters to clear my credentials, is pleased to show me the vessel's state-of-the-art navigation system.

A computer map much like the one on your home television screen shows the weather in the region. The officers also call in regularly to the NOAA weather station at Newport, N.C., and send in their own weather reports three or four times daily.

Two hazards, the captain says, are the ever-present crab pots and the shrimp boats, which maintain relatively stationary positions as they work, in contrast to the steadily moving ferry. "The best place for the crab pots is on the slope from the shallows to the channel," he explains. If lines should foul the ferryboat's propellers, the crew would have to get a diver to go under and make repairs in port.

The crew on this route work twelve hours on, ttwelve hours off for seven-day shifts, alternating with seven days off. Their morning routine begins with the deck personnel checking to see that the boat is ready: they start the generators (after the boat has been connected to shore electricity at night) and get the main engines going. The chief calls up to the pilot house, which then takes control of the vessel. The captain fires up the electronic gear—radars, depth finder, radio, and the like.

Up on the bridge, the officers have a clear view on nearly all sides and an impressive array of instruments. There are two steering systems (really four, since the boat can be steered with a lever if needed). There is also an alarm system for the boat's below-deck compartments, to show which are open. The computer-screen chart is connected to GPS, which records position dynamically throughout the passage. Fancy electronics notwithstanding, the captain still keeps a paper log.

The boat is powered by two 850-horsepower main engines, capable of delivering a speed of 12.5 knots. Averaging 10 knots, it takes 550 gallons of diesel fuel per day to make four crossings. "You burn more fuel if you have to run harder, just like a car," explains Captain Mason.

Engineer R. A. Graham comes into the pilot house and joins the conversation. How about night navigation? I ask the men. There are buoys to mark the channel, they explain, but the crew also rely on radar. Powerful lamps can be directed toward water or land as needed, and help in docking after dark.

When it comes to dealing with passengers, the crew have learned through years of experience what to watch out for. If a driver is gripping the steering wheel tightly with both hands, says mate W. G. Mason, that's bad. "You see their muscles tense up." He rolls his eyes to indicate the potential consequences. "Or you see them driving up talking on their cell phones."

Other onboard difficulties include dead batteries—as when a traveler leaves the car radio on for two hours. But by far the most common problem is keys locked in the car. "I hear car alarms go off," says the captain. "My mind is attuned to anything out of the ordinary." And he's gone so far as to get on the PA system and remind his passengers, "Nobody will steal your car on this ferry"—or if they do, they won't get very far.

I ask what kind of vehicles the ferry can transport. "Most people don't realize what's involved" in the ferries' cargo, says W. G. Mason. Captain Mason chimes in: "After Hurricane Isabel, we had to bring over everything that was needed on the island for repairs: big trucks, rocks, everything." The Sound Class ferries can carry 300 passengers, but vehicle capacity varies depending on the type of vehicles. Fuel trucks, for instance, still have to call ahead to get clearance for a special run, and military convoys arrange transportation in advance.

Mate Mason can't resist another anecdote. He parrots the British accent of one passenger who approached him and said, "I'm afraid I've locked my keys in my car." The crew offered assistance in jimmying the lock, but to no avail. The passenger studied the situation for a moment. "Is that your chief stoker?" he asked Mr. Mason, referring to the engineer.

"Have him take a hammer and knock the window out," the man directed, resigning himself to the necessity. "I don't mind paying to have it replaced, but it sure buggers the air conditioning."

etc.) and safety features of ferries and other marine vessels in general, consult *Principles of Naval Architecture,* edited by John M. Comstock (Society of Naval Architects and Marine Engineers, 1967).

Crew and training

Sound Class vessels are staffed by a crew of six: a master, a chief engineer, a mate, and an oiler, plus one able seaman and one ordinary seaman. Hatteras Class boats are run by a crew of five, River Class by a crew of four. Overall, the state Ferry Division employs approximately 400 men and women during the winter season and 500 during the summer; other ferries throughout the state account for dozens more positions.

All ferry crew members are either documented or licensed by the Coast Guard, according to a strict system of advancement in their field. Ordinary seamen, the term for entry-level licensees whether male or female, serve as deckhands; after more experience they may take an examination to qualify as able-bodied (AB) seamen. Oilers work as assistant engineers; engineers, the next step up, are licensed for the horsepower of a particular ferry and the waters in which it operates. Mates are licensed and in training to be masters; and masters, who are licensed for the size vessel and area of operation, are qualified to be in charge of their own boat.

Securing a position on a ferry crew takes dedication and professionalism. To begin with, applying for and obtaining Coast Guard documents often takes several months. After that, advancement to the next level requires considerable on-the-job training—a minimum of two years between levels, often involving completion of further Coast Guard courses. By the time a ferry operator qualifies as master or chief engineer, he or she has amassed an impressive record of skill and knowledge. Though they tend to be modest about their experience, ferry crews have on more than one occasion been responsible for assisting stranded boaters or rescuing vessels in distress.

Ferry Division employees are often retired military, while some come to the ferry service from the private-sector marine industry. But most start with the ferry service and work their way up the ladder. Just a glance at the employment roster shows a host of family names long associated with fishing and boating on the Carolina coast.

The ferry operations rely on a qualified staff at shore facilities as well: an operation manager; lead clerks, who deal with all paperwork; processing assistants, who sell tickets and memorabilia in addition to tickets; and general utility workers, who do maintenance and whatever else is needed.

Ferry tales

When it comes to onboard situations, ferry employees have seen it all. On the Southport–Fort Fisher run, there's a regular commuter who does tai chi every morning "like clockwork." And there are couples who "get kind of amorous," Southport crew member Steve Smith says. "They forget that there are people up top who can see right into their cars."

River ferries are driven by onboard diesel motors and guided on course by a steel cable secured on each bank.

There are some folks who walk on, bring a picnic onboard, and casually bring out the wine in plastic cups. There are people who get out on deck and dance. A group of construction workers and fishermen passes the time with a friendly game of Texas Hold 'Em on the long Cedar-Island–Ocracoke crossing.

The ferry employees are a patient and philosophical lot, coolly dealing with the unexpected on any given crossing.

Cable-guided river ferries

The two-car river ferryboat operates on an entirely different basis: no timetable, no reservations, no crowds, no fancy GPS.

Tethered to a steel cable stretched across the breadth of the river (a bit like the rope that divides lanes of a swimming pool), the ferry travels forward and back from bank to bank. It carries two vehicles at a time on its flat deck, loading from either end and unloading from the opposite one on hydraulically controlled ramps. Signs warn boaters about the cable during ferry hours, so that they can take caution as they pass under. Larger vessels must call ahead and ask the ferry operator to lower the cable to the bottom for passage.

A diesel engine mounted on the side provides power, and a one-person booth serves as the wheelhouse.

The operator generally docks the boat on the riverbank where the shore facility is located. Vehicles arriving on the opposite side signal for the ferry by honking their horns—the boat crosses over, loads, and returns to the other side, all within the space of a few minutes' time.

The river ferries operate from dawn to dusk, as long as high water or lightning don't prevent them from running. When darkness falls and the ferry's day is over, the operator runs a shore-mounted winch to lower the cable to the bottom of the river

Drivers wishing to ride the river ferries must signal the operator if the boat is docked in the opposite shore.

for the night.

On shallow waters or deep, North Carolina's dependable ferries carry their loads with grace, power, and the fascinating evidences of human ingenuity.

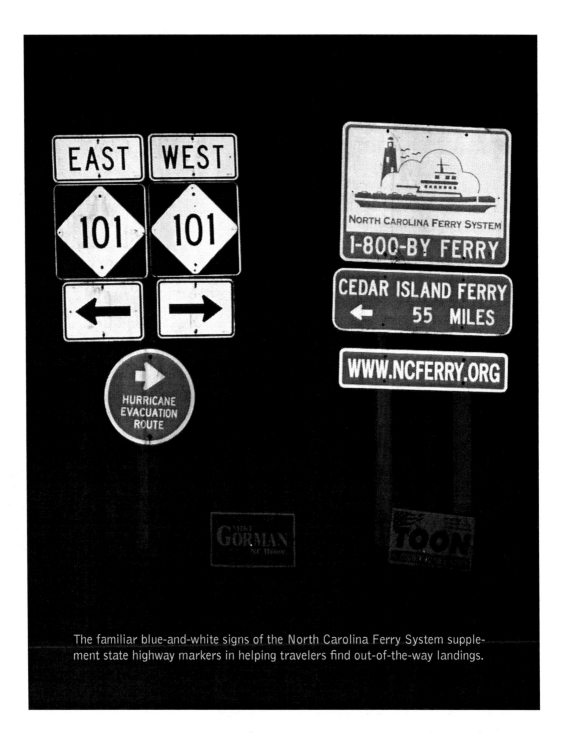

The familiar blue-and-white signs of the North Carolina Ferry System supplement state highway markers in helping travelers find out-of-the-way landings.

the **ferry** experience: helpful hints for **travelers**

THE WOMAN IN THE CORVETTE that was first in line steered tentatively across the loading ramp, one eye nervously on the crew member who was waving her forward and the other on the rail of the boat. She nosed the car into position at the bow, cut the engine, and set the parking brake. The crewman positioning chocks under the wheels could see, however, that something was still bothering her. "Just one more thing," she asked him. "Will I have to back all the way off the boat when we get to the other side?"

If you're a rookie on your first car ferry passage, relax—the answer is no. All the driver had to do upon unloading was to release the brake, crank the car, and drive up the gently sloping off-ramp—and she was relieved to know she'd be on her way again.

But there's lots you might not know about the ferry experience. So whether you're preparing for a long cruise across the sound or are hopping across the river, read on. Several of the state's ferries are passenger-only, mind you—read each chapter in detail before planning your trip.

Vehicle loading and unloading are simple, well-orchestrated procedures. Licensed personnel will guide you through everything

you need to do. When you drive your car through the gates to the landing, you'll pull up to the ticket window (if a toll applies) and then into the assigned loading lane. Vehicles of all sizes—from motorcycles to motor homes, pickup trucks to dump trucks—travel on the vehicle ferries. Leave your vehicle parked in its place in the lane if you have

The first car loaded on will be the first off when the shore ramp is lowered.

time for a restroom stop, a trip to the vending machines, or even a picnic on shore; loading begins five to ten minutes before departure. If you leave the lane in your vehicle, you risk losing your place in line altogether.

When driving the back roads that lead to the isolated **river ferries**, be watchful for high water on the road or at the riverbank. When you board (the ferries carry only two cars at a time), drive forward especially slowly—on rare occasions vehicles have gone right on past the chain and off the front end! Take care in driving off as well; the access ramp may be steep, like a boat ramp, and the ferry's apron simply lowers to an angle that meets it. (Note an important restriction: the Department of Transportation reminds drivers that RVs cannot travel on the cable ferries.)

On the larger boats, it takes a surprisingly short time for the crew to load twenty or more vehicles. When it's time, the crew will lower the on-ramp, raise the barrier, and motion drivers onto the boat. (Pedestrians and bicyclists are generally asked to board and disembark after vehicles, for safety as well as efficiency.) Drive straight forward into the lane indicated; you'll be packed in pretty close to other vehicles, and when you turn off your engine and set the parking brake, you'll need to stay in your vehicle until loading is completed and the captain sounds the horn to indicate the vessel is under way.

On deck. Once the horn sounds you're free to **get out and move about the boat** (this is true even on the small river ferries, though there's not much deck to walk on). During the school year, children transported to school via ferry remain inside the lounge area, under the supervision of a chaperon.

If you have **pets in the car**, make sure to leave the windows cracked for ventilation

Summer afternoons can get crowded on the state ferry routes—reservations will ensure a place on the Outer Banks ferries.

and keep a close check—especially in the heat of summer. Pets are permitted on the North Carolina state ferries as long as they are either in the vehicle or on a leash. (On the private ferries going to barrier islands, rules about pets vary. Check first.)

The vehicle deck, the enclosed passenger lounge, and upper observation decks are fair game for exploration. Don't venture beyond the barriers at the bow and stern, however, or attempt to go below decks, up to the bridge, or into any other area marked restricted.

Security is a heightened concern on ferries just as on any other public transportation since 9/11. Although ferry passengers aren't generally asked for identification, the law does require you to show valid ID if official personnel request it and to otherwise cooperate with instructions of the crew.

So—what to do while on board? Sound crossings to the Outer Banks take more than two hours, so you'll be spending a substantial stretch of time aboard. The coastal river crossings and the island-hop from Ocracoke to Hatteras last from 20 to 40 minutes. On the cable-guided river ferries, there's no need to plan on a leisurely cruise; the trip requires only about five minutes.

Well, you could always sleep—in your vehicle or on a soft bench in the lounge. But why, when you could . . .

1. **Feed the seagulls.** Technically you're not supposed to do this—but if you must, please conduct your activities only at the stern.

2. **Take photos.** If you think there's nothing but sky and water when you're out in the middle of Pamlico Sound, take a look around the boat itself. Colors, textures, and light surprise at every turn. Passengers are an ever-changing cast of characters. And some days you'll get lucky with the sunrises and sunsets, or pass another vessel midway.

3. **Talk to the crew.** Between duties, they're always willing to answer questions, tell stories, or just chat. They are a knowledgeable and professional bunch.

4. **Play video games in the arcade.** The noise will annoy everyone else, but if you're really into it, you won't notice.

The privately run *Patriot* carries passengers—but no motor vehicles—to Bald Head Island in Brunswick County.

5. **Watch television in the lounge.** If you're experiencing media withdrawal already, just wait till you reach the Outer Banks beaches.

Some routes tune the onboard TV set to the GPS chart, so you can monitor the boat's progress just as the captain does.

6. **Talk on your cell phone**—if you absolutely must—for as long as you remain

If you must feed the gulls, do so only from the stern!

in range. But keep the phone turned off during loading and unloading to avoid interference with crew communications.

7. **Go to the bathroom.** Restroom facilities (the head, if you aren't familiar with nautical jargon) are available on the vehicle-deck level on the larger boats. Shore restroom facilities provide handicapped access.

8. **Read** the travel brochures, onboard newspaper, history plaques, license, and inspection documents. Or bring along a trashy novel, a comic book, or the Sunday paper.

9. **Look through the bag of goodies you purchased in the Ship's Store at the landing:** NC Ferries T-shirt, coloring book, cap, deck of cards, coffee mug, toy binoculars, pen and pencil, keychain . . . .

10. **Fill up your coffee cup** (on most routes)—$1 donation to the kitty, or free if you brought your NC Ferries mug with you.

11. **Visit** with other passengers. Get to know new friends from all over.

12. **Bring a picnic** to enjoy in your car, up top, or in the lounge. Plain or fancy, food and beverage are a great accompaniment to the breeze and the view. And just in case you were wondering about the wine: the state's official policy is that the ferries are an extension of the highway—subject to all relevant regulations about open containers and DUI.

13. **Purchase sodas and crackers, candy, or other snacks** from onboard vending machines if you forgot the picnic basket.

14. **Play cards or a board game** with the kids. Or if you came alone, play solitaire. Most of the lounge areas are equipped with booths and tables.

15. **Catch up on your spreadsheets** on your laptop while your kids pass the time with their GameBoys.

16. **Plot your position on a GPS device.** If your coordinates come up outside a boundary of 33 to 37 degrees north latitude and 75 to 80 degrees west longitude, get a differ-

ent book—you're in the wrong state.

17. **Look for dolphins, fish, birds, and other wildlife**. See which species you can identify.

18. On the way back, **write letters and postcards** describing your trip. (Be sure and send one to the author of this book at ferrytales@ferriesofnorthcarolina.com.)

19. **Lean over the rail** (careful, not too far) and watch the water rushing by. Keep your keys safely in your pocket and your camera secured by a strap.

20. **Smoke** (not recommended)—but only on the rear upper deck, never in your vehicle or on the vehicle deck. On some ferries, smoking is not allowed.

21. **Sit in your car** the entire time with windows rolled up and doors locked, not moving for two hours, and pretend it's morning rush hour in Los Angeles.

A few reminders will ensure that you have a safe, enjoyable, and convenient trip. For motor vehicles, **reservations** are often necessary to ensure a spot on the Cedar Island and Swan Quarter routes to and from Ocracoke during high season (Memorial Day to late September), and recommended at other times. You may make a reservation by toll-free phone, or in person at the ferry terminal; you pay by credit card or cash (no checks) when you arrive for departure. The state ferry system now also makes discount passes available for frequent travelers as well.

You must arrive at least 30 minutes ahead of time to claim your reservation. In high season, and especially if you hope to return to the mainland on a Sunday afternoon, it's a smart idea to make your return reservation at the same time you make your outbound one.

Phone numbers for each route are listed in the ferry system schedule brochure and in this book and many other travel guides. But if those happen not to be handy, the easy-to-remember toll-free number 1.800.BY-

At the Hatteras Inlet landing, a new visitor center features a lounge with snack and drink vending and a Ship's Store.

FERRY will provide the reservations numbers and other information.

Slightly different procedures apply for the private ferries—call ahead or visit their websites for details.

The ferry crossing provides a refreshing respite for the road-weary traveler.

Bicycles are always welcome on the state ferries, as are **travelers on foot**. If you plan to walk on, and you're arriving at one of the more isolated terminals, make sure transportation is available to your destination. (The Southport terminal, for instance, is two miles from town. On Bald Head Island, if you expect to venture farther than the marina village, you'll need to make arrangements for bikes or golf carts.)

If you leave your car on deck and decide to lock your vehicle, check before locking to make sure your **keys** are in a secure place on your person and not inside the vehicle. (Keys lost overboard or locked in cars are the top passenger problem ferry crews are called on to address.)

If you should become **ill or injured** onboard, notify a crew member. First aid is available on board, and the crew can obtain help in more serious situations as well. Seasickness is extremely rare among passengers on the calm waters of North Carolina's rivers and sounds, but travelers prone to any sort of motion sickness might do well to prepare with medication or other precautionary therapy. Accidents involving falling overboard are even rarer; but ferry personnel are fully trained in procedures for promptly dealing with any such eventuality. (You might be interested to know that "rail-jumping" off any public vessel is against Coast Guard regulations, regardless of the intent or skill level of the diver.)

What should you bring with you if you're taking a ferry to the islands? That depends as much on the particular destination as on whether you're driving a 24-foot RV or a Miata. When you're visiting Hammocks Beach or Cape Lookout, for example, everything you need for your stay (including water) must be carried in, and trash must be carried out. In either case, and at any time of year, bring sunscreen if you plan to spend time on the open ferry deck or the beach. Bug spray is a necessity for beachgoing and camping on the islands in all but the coolest weather.

Dress is simple, casual, and practical — layers will help you prepare for fluctuations in temperature while allowing you to travel light. In cooler weather you'll need a jacket onboard the ferry. Rain is always a possibility on any of the crossings, and not all of the vehicle decks are covered—so maneuvering between your car and the lounge might call for a slicker.

As for clothes-changing, shower, and toilet facilities once you're on the islands, amenities vary widely—from five-star resorts to portable toilets to, well, the latrine shovel. You should consult a general travel guide particular to your destination, especially if you're day-tripping to the beaches. (Glenn Morris's *North Carolina Beaches,* in an updated 2005 edition by the University of North Carolina Press, is comprehensive; the *Insider's Guides* are also very good.)

Restroom facilities, including access for the handicapped, are available at all state ferry terminals; at private terminals, options vary.

Almost all of the state terminals are equipped with food and drink vending machines, and some provide coffee and snacks. Many vessels have vending services onboard as well (none serve meals of any sort, however).

The North Carolina Ferry Division has steadily worked to improve **shore facilities** at all its terminals. In addition to restrooms and vending machines, many also have clean, inviting visitors' centers and lounges, pay phones, and water fountains. Most of the ferry landings, state-owned or private, are furnished with picnic tables and grassy lawns for travelers' enjoyment.

Parking at the state terminals is free of charge. Be aware that access gates to ferry landings are locked after the last arrival or departure, since none of the routes operates round the clock.

Motel accommodations are available within walking distance of both terminals of

If you miss the last ferry . . . better know where to find accommodations nearby.

the Cedar Island–Ocracoke run, and if your departure should be canceled or you miss your ferry you may find yourself grateful for a "Vacancy" sign. If you're stuck at any of the other landings, however, don't count on overnight lodgings closer than the next town down the road.

Gas for your car is another commodity not always readily accessible near the ferry terminals. Fill up well beforehand.

One last word of caution. It's true that **vehicle mishaps** do sometimes occur. Cars have been known to run out of fuel and fail to restart; engines have been known to stall;

keys have gotten lost; minor door-scrapes and fender-benders have sometimes happened. Prevention and watchfulness are the best approaches—but if any of these situations should befall your car, rest assured the dedicated ferry personnel won't leave you stranded. Find the nearest crew member and ask for assistance.

However you spend your time on the ferry passage, the opposite shore comes into view all too soon. The captain steers into the channel and makes an announcement over the loudspeaker when it's time for drivers to return to their vehicles. The ferry will pull into port with cars facing the dock's paved access ramp. When the horn sounds that the boat is safely at the dock, crank your engine again and release your parking brake, and follow the crew's directions onto the ramp. In dark or rain, keep your headlights off until you cross the ramp to avoid blinding loading personnel or traffic waiting to board.

As you look back at the boat's fading lights in the distance, and the sun rises or sets over the glimmering water as you turn onto the highway and head for the beach, maybe you'll count yourself lucky for a travel experience far outside the ordinary. And maybe, if you're even luckier, you'll get to make the return trip in a few days—on the ferry again, just like you came.

Sunset over Pamlico Sound

the NC **state ferry** system

THE NORTH CAROLINA FERRY DIVISION was established in 1947 as part of the state Highway Department, itself a part of the Department of Transportation. At the time it operated only one route and subsidized a few others, which had grown to seven by 1977. No other route has been added or discontinued since then (recent plans for a passegner ferry service from Currituck to Corolla have been postponed indefinitely).

These days, the NC ferry system moves more than 1 million vessels and 2 million passengers per year. It manages 24 boats (the newest one, M/V *Hatteras,* put into service in 2006), plus various support craft and a dredge. It also maintains a headquarters in Morehead City and the North Carolina State Shipyard at Manns Harbor, in Dare County.

The Ferry Division, according to its literature, "is dedicated to providing safe, cost effective and dependable service for the traveling public." The Ferry Division's mission is accomplished by:

• Ensuring that its vessels are operated and maintained to the highest levels of maritime safety.

• Promoting customer satisfaction by providing information, education, a comfortable environment,

and other amenities to achieve a favorable traveling experience.

• Operating all vessels and shore establishments with professionally competent, courteous, and knowledgeable employees.

• Affording all available resources to aid residents and visitors in response to natural or man-made disasters.

The Ferry System also

• aids in hurricane evacuation and relief provides a positive economic impact by bringing tourists to Eastern North Carolina;

• works closely with commercial, civic, religious and state organizations.

A bankside picnic is an enjoyable way to wait for the ferry's arrival.

The North Carolina state ferry fleet

Ferryboats in the state's fleet are listed here by class. Statistics and university affiliation are listed for each vessel, as well as the route it customarily serves. Vessels may be reassigned or operated on different routes than the ones listed if needed to handle extra capacity, or in case a boat is out for repair.

SOUND CLASS

Carteret
Route	Cedar Island–Ocracoke
Capacity	50 vehicles, 300 passengers
Crew	6
Gross tonnage	771
Length	220'6"
Breadth	51'
Depth	12.781'
Draft	5.05' (light), 6'6" (loaded)
Engines	(2) Cat 3508 (805hp each)
Built	1989, Halter Marine; 59' 6"midbody added and superstructure rebuilt 1998
Affiliation	UNC–Chapel Hill
Colors	Carolina blue/white

Cedar Island
Route	Cedar Island–Ocracoke
Capacity	50 vehicles, 300 passengers
Crew	6
Gross tonnage	648
Length	220'6"
Breadth	50'
Depth	12'6"
Draft	5'2" (light), 6'6" (loaded)
Engines	(2) Cat 3508 (805hp each)
Built	1994, Trinity Marine Group (Moss Point Marine)
Affiliation	East Carolina University
Colors	Purple/gold

Governor Edward Hyde
Route	Ocracoke–Swan Quarter
Capacity	35 vehicles, 300 passengers
Crew	6
Gross tonnage	574

Length	161'
Breadth	48'
Depth	12'6"
Draft	6.485' (light), 7.42' (loaded)
Engines	(2) Cat D398 (825hp each)
Built	1977, Equitable Shipyards, New Orleans
Affiliation	Western Carolina University
Colors	Purple/gold

Silver Lake
Route	Cedar Island–Ocracoke
Capacity	50 vehicles, 300 passengers
Crew	6
Gross tonnage	688
Length	220'6"
Breadth	48'
Depth	12'6"
Draft	5.5' (light), 6' (loaded)
Engines	(2) Cat 3508 (805hp each)
Built	1965, New Bern Shipyard; 59'6"midbody added 1987; new superstructure added 2002
Affiliation	UNC–Charlotte
Colors	Green/white

Pamlico
Route	Cedar Island–Ocracoke
Capacity	50 vehicles, 300 passengers
Crew	6
Gross tonnage	734
Length	220'6"
Breadth	48'
Depth	12'6"
Draft	5.5' (light), 6' (loaded)
Engines	(2) Cat 3508 (805hp each)
Built	1965, New Bern Shipyard; 59'6"midbody added 1986; new superstructure added 2003
Affiliation	NC School of the Arts
Colors	Teal blue/white

HATTERAS CLASS

Cape Point
Route	Ocracoke–Hatteras
Capacity	30 vehicles, 149 passengers
Crew	4
Gross tonnage	275
Length	151'9"

Breadth 42'
Depth 8'6"
Draft 4' (loaded)
Engines (2) Cat 3408 (443hp each)
Built 1989/90, Patti Shipyard, Pensacola, Fla.
Affiliation NC A&T State University
Colors Royal blue/gold

Chicamacomico
Route Ocracoke–Hatteras
Capacity 30 vehicles, 149 passengers
Crew 4
Gross tonnage 275
Length 149'9"
Breadth 42'
Depth 8'6"
Draft 4' (loaded)
Engines (2) Cat 3408 (443hp each)
Built 1989/90, Patti Shipyard, Pensacola, Fla.
Affiliation UNC–Asheville
Colors Blue/white

Frisco
Route Ocracoke–Hatteras
Capacity 30 vehicles, 149 passengers
Crew 4
Gross tonnage 275.9
Length 149'9"
Breadth 42'
Depth 8'6"
Draft 4' (loaded)
Engines (2) Cat 3408 (443hp each)
Built 1989/90, Patti Shipyard, Pensacola, Fla.
Affiliation Appalachian State University
Colors Black/gold

Hatteras
Route Ocracoke–Hatteras
Capacity 40 vehicles, 300 passengers
Crew 6
Gross tonnage 417
Length 180'
Breadth 44'
Depth 11'
Draft 6' (loaded)
Engines (2) CAT 3412 (475hp each)
Built 2006
Affiliation Shaw University
Colors Garnet/white

Ship's Stores offer a variety of gifts, toys, apparel, souvenirs, books, and other merchandise for customers

Herbert C. Bonner
Route Cherry Branch–Minnesott Beach
Capacity 22 vehicles, 100 passengers
Crew 4
Gross tonnage 199.33
Length 122'
Breadth 40'
Depth 8'6"
Draft 3'6" (loaded)
Engines (2) Detroit 6-71 (165hp each)
Built 1970, New Bern Shipyard
Affiliation Elon College
Colors Gold/maroon

Kinnakeet

Route	Ocracoke–Hatteras
Capacity	30 vehicles, 149 passengers
Crew	4
Gross tonnage	280.98
Length	151'9"
Breadth	42'
Depth	8'6"
Draft	4' (loaded)
Engines	(2) Cat 3408 (443hp each)
Built	1989, Houma Fabricators, Houma, La.
Affiliation	Elizabeth City State University
Colors	Blue/white

Ocracoke

Route	Ocracoke–Hatteras
Capacity	30 vehicles, 149 passengers
Crew	4
Gross tonnage	275.9
Length	149'9"
Breadth	42'
Depth	8'6"
Draft	4' (loaded)
Engines	(2) Cat 3408 (443hp each)
Built	1989/90, PTrinity Marine Group, Gulfport, Miss.
Affiliation	Elon College
Colors	Gold/maroon

Roanoke

Former *Floyd J. Lupton;* name changed Feb. 2000

Route	Cherry Branch–Minnesott Beach
Capacity	30 vehicles, 149 passengers
Crew	4
Gross tonnage	248
Length	149'9"
Breadth	42'
Depth	8'6"
Draft	4' (loaded)
Engines	(2) Cat 3408 (475hp each)
Built	1993, Steiner Shipyard, Bayou La Batre, Ala.
Affiliation	Meredith College
Colors	Maroon/white

Thomas A. Baum

Route	Ocracoke–Hatteras
Capacity	30 vehicles, 149 passengers
Crew	4
Gross tonnage	248
Length	149'9"
Breadth	42'
Depth	8'6"

Draft	4' (loaded)
Engines	(2) Cat 3408 (475hp each)
Built	1995, Steiner Shipyard, Bayou La Batre, Ala.
Affiliation	NC State University
Colors	Red/white

RIVER CLASS

Croatoan

Route	Ocracoke–Hatteras
Capacity	40 vehicles, 300 passengers
Crew	5
Gross tonnage	376
Length	180'
Breadth	44'
Depth	11"
Draft	5'6" (light), 6' (loaded)
Engines	(2) Cat 3412 (475hp each)
Built	2002/03, Steiner Shipyard, Bayou La Batre, Ala. Voith-Schneider propulsion
Affiliation	Methodist College
Colors	Green/yellow

Floyd J. Lupton

Route	Cherry Branch–Minnesott Beach
Capacity	40 vehicles, 300 passengers
Crew	6
Gross tonnage	374/437
Length	180'
Breadth	44'
Depth	11"
Draft	5'6" (light), 6' (loaded)
Engines	(2) Cat 3412 (475hp each)
Built	1999/2000, Halter Moss Point, Escatawpa, Miss. Voith-Schneider propulsion
Affiliation	UNC–Pembroke
Colors	Black/gold

Fort Fisher

Route	Southport–Ft. Fisher
Capacity	40 vehicles, 300 passengers
Crew	6
Gross tonnage	374/437
Length	180'
Breadth	44'
Depth	11"
Draft	5'6" (light), 6' (loaded)
Engines	(2) Cat 3412 (475hp each)
Built	1999/2000, Halter Moss Point,

Escatawpa, Miss.
Voith-Schneider propulsion
Affiliation UNC Wilmington
Colors Green/gold

Governor Daniel Russell

Route Aurora–Bayview
Capacity 40 vehicles, 300 passengers
Crew 6
Gross tonnage 418.37
Length 180'
Breadth 44'
Depth 11"
Draft 5'6" (light), 6' (loaded)
Engines (2) Cat 3412 (475hp each)
Built 1992/93, Orange Shipbuilding, Orange, Tex.
Double-ended with propellers
Affiliation Gardner-Webb University
Colors Black/red

Governor James B. Hunt

Route Currituck–Knotts Island
Capacity 22 vehicles, 149 passengers
Crew 5
Gross tonnage 462
Length 159'3"
Breadth 40'
Depth 8'6"
Draft 5' (loaded)
Engines (2) Cat 3412 (425hp each)
Built 1984, Offshore Shipbuilding, Palatka, Fla.; 29'9" midbody added 1999
Affiliation UNC–Greensboro
Colors Purple/gold

Neuse

Route Cherry Branch–Minnesott Beach
Capacity 40 vehicles, 300 passengers
Crew 5
Gross tonnage 374
Length 180'
Breadth 44'
Depth 11"
Draft 5'6" (light), 6' (loaded)
Engines (2) Cat 3412 (475hp each)
Built 1997/98, Steiner Shipyard, Bayou La Batre, Ala.
Voith-Schneider propulsion
Affiliation Wake Forest University
Colors Black/gold

Southport

Route Southport–Ft. Fisher
Capacity 40 vehicles, 300 passengers
Crew 6
Gross tonnage 424
Length 180'
Breadth 44'
Depth 11"
Draft 5'6" (light), 6' (loaded)
Engines (2) Cat 3412 (475hp each)
Built 1995/96, Steiner Shipyard, Bayou La Batre, Ala.
Voith-Schneider propulsion
Affiliation Duke University
Colors Royal blue

W. Stanford White

Route Ocracoke–Hatteras
Capacity 40 vehicles, 300 passengers
Crew 5
Gross tonnage 372
Length 180'
Breadth 44'
Depth 11"
Draft 5'6" (light), 6' (loaded)
Engines (2) Cat 3412 (475hp each)
Built 2002/03, Orange Shipbuilding, Orange, Tex.
Voith-Schneider propulsion
Affiliation Winston-Salem State University
Colors Red/white

FORT FISHER
MOREHEAD CITY NC

Southport– Fort Fisher SCHEDULE

ALL DATES AND TIMES
SUBJECT TO CHANGE
CALL 1.800.BY-FERRY

Map and directions, pp. 46–47

Departs Fort Fisher	Departs Southport
----	5.30 am
6.15 am	----
----	7.00 am
7.45 am	7.45 am
8.30 am	8.30 am
9.15 am	9.15 am
10.00 am	*10.00 am
*10.45 am	10.45 am
11.30 am	11.30 am
12.15 pm	*12.15 pm
*1.00 pm	1.00 pm
1.45 pm	1.45 pm
2.30 pm	2.30 pm
3.15 pm	3.15 pm
4.00 pm	4.00 pm
4.45 pm	4.45 pm
5.30 pm	----
----	6.15 pm
7.00 pm	----
	* Summer runs only: April 3 – Oct 1, 2007

Crossing the Cape Fear River from Southport, the ferry approaches the Fort Fisher landing

STOP

Headlights OFF

CHAPTER 1

Southport– Fort Fisher

vehicle/passenger ferry

route Crosses mouth of Cape Fear River from **Southport** (pop. 2,605, Brunswick County) to Federal Point, near Fort Fisher State Recreation Area and State Historic Site (nearest town **Kure Beach,** pop. 1,858, New Hanover County)

duration 30 min

distance 3 mi

vessels River Class (34–36 vehicles, 300 passengers): M/V *Southport*; M/V *Fort Fisher*

fare One way
Pedestrian $1.00
Bicycle rider $2.00
Motorcycle $3.00
Vehicle and/or combination less than 20′ $5.00
Vehicle and/or combination 20′ up to 40′ $10.00
Vehicle and/or combination over 40′ up to 65′ $15.00

reservations No

terminal Southport
Ferry Rd. SE, Southport NC 28461
1.800.368.8969
910.457.6942
Fort Fisher
Fort Fisher Rd. S, Kure Beach NC 28449
910.458.3229

shore facilities Fort Fisher: Restrooms, picnic tables, vending machines
Southport: Visitor center with offices, Ship's Store, restrooms, vending machines

fact Southport–Fort Fisher is the only ferry route from which one can view three lighthouses simultaneously: Bald Head Island, Oak Island, and Price's Creek.

A FERRY TRIP TO SOUTHPORT FOR *Father's Day seems like the perfect solution on a ninety-four-degree June day when no one can muster much enthusiasm for the beach—though the Brannons, it seems, aren't the only ones with this bright idea.*

Driving down from Wilmington, we pull into the long line at the Fort Fisher landing about noon. The 12:15 departure is full. On top of that, the ticket clerk tells us, the 1:00 has been cancelled—an infrequent occurrence on this route. Nothing wrong with the boat mechanically, he says, but a minor

safety issue has to be checked out, so they're running only one vessel this afternoon.

We wait for the 12:15 boat to load, then purchase our ticket for the 1:45. The car ahead of us thinks better of the wait, so we're first in line at the gate and conveniently adjacent to the picnic shelter.

Southport's yacht basin welcomes recreational boats and fishing vessels.

Why not just have our lunch here? We unload the picnic gear—grill and all—and proceed to cook our meal dockside, even if it's so windy we have to weight everything down.

But it's an enjoyable meal, and it's lots less crowded here than at the state park up the road. My father, who was stationed at Fort Fisher Air Force Station in the 1950s, recalls when there was no ferry here—nor much of anything else.

We're finishing off the last bites of steak and burgers when we see the Southport *approaching, sporting its blue-and-white Duke colors. Dessert will have to wait till the other side.*

The crew prepare to load vehicles up to capacity, fitting everyone in expertly, then bringing the bicyclists and foot passengers aboard. As we drive on, the deckhand, Mr. Haselden by his badge, takes note of the chocolate cake my sister carries in her lap, its homemade frosting glistening in the midday sun. "My favorite!" he jokes.

Everybody's having fun, dads and kids of all ages reveling in the cooling wind and water. Among the crew is a relative newcomer, Wilmington retiree Harold Peterson. The father of the city's former mayor, Peterson started part-time work on the ferries a few weeks earlier.

From the deck, passengers can see Zeke's Island and the partly submerged jetty (the Rocks) leading to it. We pass the three lighthouses: the Civil-War era lighthouse at Price's Creek to starboard, Old Baldy on Bald Head Island to

port, and the slender Oak Island lighthouse dead ahead. The ship-loading cranes at the Sunny Point military installation, the green margin of the riverbank, and passing watercraft provide plenty of diversion, and the crossing goes quickly.

At Southport's Waterfront Park, we polish off about half the chocolate cake, along with a Thermos of coffee. On the return trip, the tide's coming in, and we spy parents and kids hopping from rock to rock, coming back from Zeke's Island before the rising water cuts them off.

Back at the Fort Fisher landing, it seems too short a day when it's time to disembark. Grill and coolers and leftovers are all packed away. Except the last half of the chocolate cake, which I hand over to Haselden as we crank the motor and wait our turn to exit.

"Hey, thanks," he says, surprise registering on his face. "You sure?"

"Of course," I answer back. "You're somebody's father too, aren't you?"

He takes the cake and waves us on.

SINCE ITS ADDITION to the state ferry system in 1965, the Southport–Fort Fisher route has been one of the state's most popular ferry runs. Today it is the fastest-growing route, in terms of rider numbers, in the system. It's going "gangbusters down there," as a Ferry Division staffer puts it.

Part of the route's popularity, without doubt, is due to its thirty-minute duration—short enough for a pleasant ride but long enough for enjoyable sightseeing—and its proximity to populated areas. Its entire route passes within sight of land, so the scenery is as changing as the parade of other boats in the channel, to the birds on the spoil islands (mandmade mounds of dredged material) of the Cape Fear River.

For Captain Marybeth Ray the route is something new every day. Growing up around boats in the Bahamas and earning her master's license in 1986, she's worked on everything from recreational boats to naval supply vessels, but here on the Cape Fear River ferry she has shared the channel with classic yachts, commercial cargo ships, and even the tall ship *Eagle*. "A twelve-and-a-half-hour day really goes very quickly," she says. "You just keep moving all day long."

In addition to boats and the changing winds and tides, Capt. Ray enjoys interacting with the passengers—though she sees less of them since moving into the captain's job in

The M/V *Fort Fisher*, sporting UNC Wilmington colors, makes the 30-minute crossing on North Carolina's fatest-growing ferry route.

2003 than she did when she worked as mate, when "you saw every car that came aboard and everybody that came aboard."

Riders and boat crews see plenty of wildlife too. Dolphins, otters, birds, and alligators are common; Capt. Ray has even spotted a deer swimming the river, to her amazement timing the heavy current just right. And then there was the round-trip bird. The crew once rescued an injured seagull on the Fort Fisher side, brought it over to Southport on the ferry, and rehabilitated it inland. When the bird was ready to be returned to its habitat after a few weeks, it was released at the Southport terminal. It calmly strolled back aboard the ferry—awaiting its ride home just the way it had arrived.

The Southport–Fort Fisher ferry draws varied riders for varied reasons: real estate agents showing waterfront property with a little razzle-dazzle. University students conducting surveys among a captive audience. Couples out for a romantic sunset cruise. Cyclists taking the scenic route. Commuters driving in from Brunswick County. Families headed for the Fourth of July parade. Even touring motorcyclists pushing for the finish line in a friendly road race: in the recent Cape Fear 1000 long-distance rally that started in Paducah, Kentucky, and ended in Wilmington, the only way to be among the top finishers was to use the ferry as a short-cut. As proof, riders were required to provide a receipt for the Southport ferry ticket.

Each end of this route offers a rich slice of history and recreation, and ample opportunities for shopping, food, and lodging. Recently improved **shore facilities** are open at each landing for the basics, and towns

(and gas and meals) are not far away.

On foot. This run gets a good number of pedestrians who do the round trip for a cheap thrill (you still have to disembark and reboard on the opposite side). But if you've traveled to the Southport side without some sort of wheels, be aware that the ferry landing is two miles from town and time your visit accordingly. On the Fort Fisher side, the ferry leaves you reasonably close to the beach and the North Carolina Aquarium— though quite a ways from town or services.

For **bicyclists,** a short ride takes you into the village of Southport, on a nicely paved bike path through pleasant tree-lined surroundings. On the Fort Fisher side, there's a

Touring biker Jim Puckett of Fruitland, Missouri, picked up bonus points for getting his ferry ticket punched on a 1,000-mile road rally in 2006.

In the pilot house of the M/V *Southport,* Captain Marybeth Ray and her crew make sixteen departures a day for eight round trips.

bike lane on NC bicycle routes 3 and 5 into Carolina Beach, as well as a shortcut from from the ferry to the aquarium—but watch for vehicles on the narrow curves.

Southport was established 1792. It is a riverfront, rather than oceanfront, town, with handsome, historic clapboard homes over-looking the water or nestled under the oaks in an orderly grid of streets (a local visual joke shows photographs of four of the town's street signs—Lord Howe Dry Iam).

The short drive into town provides a capsule of Southport's **history:** the old

Smithville Burying Ground and the mouth of the Cape Fear River, as well as Bonnet's Creek, where pirates hid their boats in more lawless days. Fort Johnston, built in 1748 on the riverfront at Iam Street, is billed as "the smallest military base in the world." Today the city pier and pleasant Waterfront Park invite visitors to enjoy a bit of fishing or boat-watching.

Southport is the kind of picture-post-card town where you'd expect American flags to fly from white-banistered porches—which, in fact, they do, year-round, but especially for

Diners on the Southport waterfront can spot watercraft of all sorts.

the Fourth of July parade. Southport puts on a jam-up Fourth celebration, as well as other events with a main-street flavor in the bandstand at Franklin Square Park.

Facilities, activites, and provisions. Not so long ago it was tough to find a place to get a bite to eat here; these days, there are dozens of restaurants, from pizza to fine dining, and a Port City Java coffee shop with Internet access. The increasing popularity of Brunswick County's year-round residential communities has made it one of the fastest-growing regions in the nation. The area's beaches, golf courses, and (previously) affordable real estate have definitely been discovered.

Galleries line the town square and Howe Street, and boutiques are tucked away in intriguing corners. Inland a ways from the center of town, there's a Wal-Mart, a Lowe's home improvement store, a bookstore, a choice of grocery stores, and an increasing array of strip-mall retailers. Provisions for long trips are readily available here 24/7. There's at least one chain motel farther inland, and several small inns that overlook the water in town.

At the yacht basin, the Southport Fishing Center is the dock for head boats and cruise boats in this area, and a great place to find seafood restaurants serving up fresh catch and live music. Downtown, the Amuzu Theater is now back in business as a performance venue. Bicycles and kayaks are available for rental at the Adventure Company on Howe Street.

Southport is also the gateway to Bald Head Island; the Indigo ferry dock is located off Howe Street at 9th (see chapter 8).

For more information

- Southport Visitors Center, 113 West Moore St., 910.454.0607
- Southport Merchants Association, www.southportmerchants.com

•

Fort Fisher, a military installation since the Civil War, occupies a neck of land at the southern tip of what's popularly called **Pleasure Island**. The island, separated from mainland New Hanover County by the artificial channel of Snow's Cut, offers vacationers everything from boating and fishing to swimming, surfing, and kayaking to dining and dancing. Even the old air force base has been repurposed as the Fort Fisher Air Force Recreation Area.

At the end of the short road off the ferry on the Fort Fisher side, turn left at the stop sign (a right turn takes you literally to the end of the road, the boat ramp, and the footpath to the Rocks and Zeke's Island).

On this stretch of road through the marsh, the mileage sign reminds you that Wilmington and US 17 lie 22 miles to the

north. The Fort Fisher State Historic Site is 1.6 miles ahead; Carolina Beach State Park, 7.5 miles (it's the closest state park to any of the ferries). But the most tantalizing sign is the one that reads "Cedar Island Ferry 151 miles." Some ferry riders who've seen that sign have asked boat crews innocently, "So, how long till we get to Cedar Island?"

The drive into Wilmington is a continually changing panorama of communities, each with its own personality. Note that the speed limit is 35 mph or lower throughout this stretch of two-lane road, until you cross the high-rise Snow's Cut bridge to the mainland, so plan your drive time accordingly. (Also note that when you're going toward the ferry

The Price's Creek Lighthouse, located on private property on the Brunswick County side of the Cape Fear River, was built in 1848.

landing, the last gas station is the TP Groceries & Gas / Fort Fisher Trading Post right outside the white gates, at 858 Hwy. 421. It's often closed during the off season; you can generally count on 24/7 gas in the heart of Carolina Beach.)

Around a sharp left curve, you'll see the glass roof of the North Carolina Aquarium, impressively rebuilt after major hurricanes of the 1990s. The entrance is 1.3 miles on the right (Loggerhead Road), which also takes you to the South End off-road access (a fee applies). In addition to its extensive indoor exhibits and educational programs, the aquarium has a large freshwater pond, several hiking trails, and an outdoor garden.

A short walk down the beach behind the aquarium takes wanderers to the WWII-era concrete bunkers like the one in which the "Fort Fisher Hermit," Robert Harrill, once lived a primitive existence for sixteen years. White-tailed deer, alligators, and shorebirds are not uncommon here.

A tall granite column at the Fort Fisher Historic Site memorializes the Civil War battles fought here. Reenactments take place here every February. Two oceanfront gazebos overlooking the dunes are popular spots for weddings; the myrtle groves and yaupon holly, shaped by wind and spray into wedges as though sheared with clippers, provide shade for picnickers. A marker reminds travelers that Confederate spy Rose Greenhow drowned near this spot. Today, below the sea-

On a chilly winter morning, visitors gather to watch the reenactment of a key Civil War battle at the Fort Fisher State Historic Site.

wall of riprap and boulders is a beach that's great for walking and fishing at low tide.

At the stop light (Ave. K) in **Kure Beach,** you can visit the Kure Beach Pier, one of the last old-style wooden fishing piers on this coast (its bait and tackle counter and gift shop are a fun step back into the past), and at the same intersection, Big Daddy's Seafood Restaurant, a longtime institution.

There are lots of affordable motels and rental houses. But the bright Bahama-colored three-story homes that now line Fort Fisher Boulevard are testimony to the booming demand for beachfront real estate at this quiet, family-oriented beach.

Carolina Beach has highrises, numerous motels, and plenty of bars and night spots. The boardwalk harkens back to an earlier era; at the corner, the art-deco Ocean Plaza, demolished in 2006, was one of the original clubs for shag dancing in the 1950s. Britt's Donuts specializes in fried doughnuts—a high-calorie, yummy treat dripping with glaze, long out of fashion elsewhere.

There's a nice walking path around the freshwater lake on Lake Park Boulevard. At the marina are dozens of head boats and the Winner family of charters. The Winners have managed boat access, real estate, and business around here since steamboat days.

Carolina Beach State Park (left at the last light before the Snow's Cut Bridge) is a great site for camping, hiking, and fishing. There's a full-service marina and a visitor center. At the bridge you'll also find a large shopping center with grocery store, drugstores, and other retail concerns.

Seabreeze, a historically black seaside resort community, is no longer in top repair, but excellent fresh seafood is available right off the boat. Turn right at Seabreeze Rd. just after the bridge on US 421.

From Seabreeze on into **Wilmington**, US 421 is four- or six-lane. At Monkey Junction (so called because of the pets a gas station owner used to keep caged there when this was a mere country crossroads), continue straight ahead for the UNCW campus and the beaches; bear left for downtown Wilmington and the riverfront.

To learn more about the region's history, take a glance at Susan Taylor Block's illustrated Arcadia volumes *Cape Fear Beaches* (2000), *Cape Fear Lost* (1999) and *Cape Fear* (2006). Page through the illustrations and anecdotes in Miller Pope's *Tales of the Silver Coast: A Secret History of North Carolina's Brunswick County* (2006). If that merely piques your curiosity for more, visit Beach Road Books on Long Beach Road outside Southport.

For more information

• Cape Fear Coast Convention and Visitors Bureau, www.cape-fear.nc.us, 1.800.641.7082; 910.341.4030
• Greater Wilmington Chamber of Commerce, www.wilmingtonchamber.org, 910.762.2611
• Pleasure Island Chamber of Commerce, www.pleasureislandnc.com or www.carolinabeach.org, 910.458.8434

Historic Southport

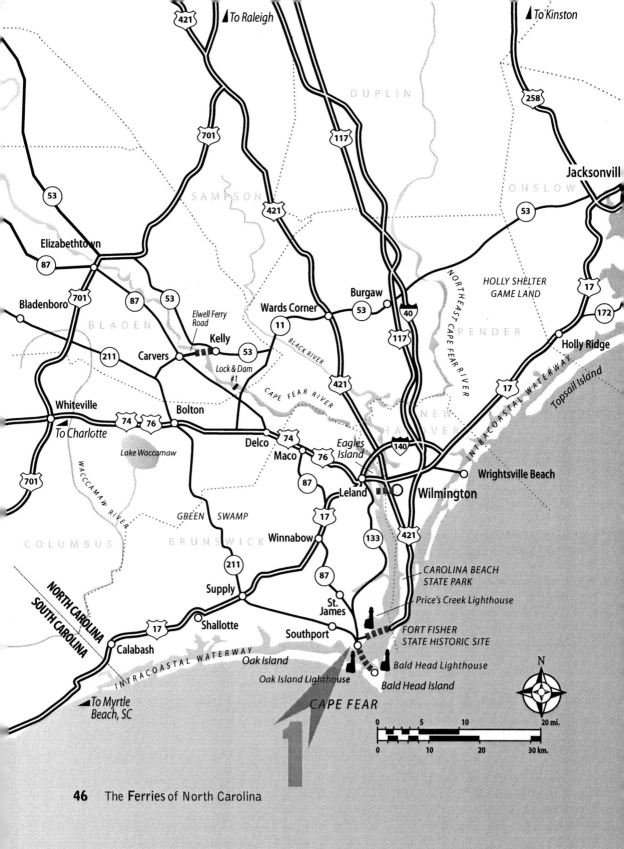

Wilmington, NC, to Southport ferry landing (west bank of Cape Fear River)

From downtown Wilmington, take US 74 W / US76 W west across the Cape Fear Memorial Bridge, for 2.7 miles. At the first exit, take the NC 133 S ramp 0.3 miles south toward Southport / Oak Island. Turn left (south) onto NC 133 / Village Rd. NE. Proceed 22.6 miles. At the intersection, stay straight to go onto NC 87 / River Rd. SE. Continue 1.2 miles, then turn left at traffic signal onto NC 211 / N. Howe St. Continue 1.5 miles, past Bald Head Island ferry entrance at 9th street, into downtown Southport. Turn left at traffic light on E. Moore St. and proceed 2.0 miles as the street curves left. Look for the blue ferry signs and turn right on Ferry Rd. SE.

Total est. distance: 30 miles
Total est. time: 50 minutes

Shallotte, NC, to Southport ferry landing (west bank of Cape Fear River)

From US 17 N / Ocean Hwy. in Shallotte, continue about 6 miles north, toward Wilmington. In the community of Supply (look for the Kangaroo convenience store), turn right (south) on NC 211 / Southport-Supply Rd.; proceed 17 miles south-east, past the St. James community, to the town of Southport, where NC 211 becomes N. Howe St. Turn left at traffic light on E. Moore St. and proceed 2.0 miles as the street curves left. Look for the blue ferry signs and turn right on Ferry Rd. SE.

Total est. distance: 25 miles
Total est. time: 35 minutes

Wilmington, NC, to Fort Fisher ferry landing (east bank of Cape Fear River)

From downtown Wilmington, take S. 3rd St. south to the intersection with Wooster St. Stay straight to go onto US 421 / Carolina Beach Rd. Continue to follow US 421 south for 22 miles, bearing left at Greenfield Park, bearing right at Monkey Junction, crossing the Snow's Cut Bridge, and passing through the towns of Carolina Beach and Kure Beach. Proceed past white gates marking Fort Fisher; pass Fort Fisher State Historic Site on right and North Carolina Aquarium entrance on left. Ferry entrance will be on right, around several sharp curves.

Total est. distance: 22 miles
Total est. time: 40 minutes, under ideal traffic conditions

The North Carolina Aquarium at Fort Fisher is one of three in the state system.

Cherry Branch– Minnesott Beach SCHEDULE

ALL DATES AND TIMES
SUBJECT TO CHANGE
CALL 1.800.BY-FERRY

Map and directions, pp. 54–55

Year-round schedule MORNING		Year-round schedule AFTERNOON / EVENING	
Departs Cherry Branch	Departs Minnesott	Departs Cherry Branch	Departs Minnesott
5.45 am	5.45 am	12.15 pm	12.15 pm
6.15 am	6.15 am	---	---
6.45 am	6.45 am	1.15 pm	1.15 pm
7.15 am	7.15 am	1.45 pm	1.45 pm
7.45 am	7.45 am	2.15 pm	2.15 pm
8.15 am	8.15 am	2.45 pm	2.45 pm
8.45 am	8.45 am	3.15 pm	3.15 pm
9.15 am	9.15 am	3.35 pm	3.35 pm
9.45 am	9.45 am	3.55 pm	3.55 pm
10.15 am	10.15 am	4.15 pm	4.15 pm
10.45 am	10.45 am	4.55 pm	4.55 pm
11.15 am	11.15 am	5.15 pm	5.15 pm
11.45 am	11.45 am	5.45 pm	5.45 pm
		---	6.15 pm
		6.45 pm	---
		---	7.15 pm
		7.45 pm	---
		---	8.15 pm
		8.45 pm	---
		---	9.15 pm
		9.45 pm	---
		---	10.15 pm
		10.45 pm	---
		---	11.15 am
		11.45 pm	---
		---	12.15 pm
		12.45 am	---

Cherry Branch–Minnesott Beach

vehicle/passenger ferry

route NC Hwy 306; crosses Neuse River from outside Havelock (pop. 22,973, Craven County) to Minnesott Beach (pop. 308, Pamlico County)

duration 20 min

distance 0.9 mi

vessels Hatteras Class (22 vehicles, 100 passengers): M/V *Herbert C. Bonner*; Hatteras Class (30 vehicles, 149 passengers): M/V *Roanoke*; River Class (40 vehicles, 300 passengers): M/V *Floyd J. Lupton*; River Class (42 vehicles, 300 passengers): M/V *Neuse*

fare Free

reservations No

terminal Cherry Branch Ferry Rd., Havelock, NC 28532
1.800.339.9156
252.447.1055
Web www.ncferry.org

shore facilities Cherry Branch: Restrooms, picnic tables, vending machines, pay telephone Minnesott Beach: covered picnic tables, vending machines, restrooms

fact This ferry route serves as a way to commute for many employees and enlisted personnel at MCAS Cherry Point.

AS WE CROSS THE WHITE OAK AND PAMLICO *Rivers and drive across the broad peninsula, isolated rainstorms have left puddles everywhere. The land is like a sponge set down into a shallow bowl of water that wells up into every low place: ditches, pocosin lakes, drainage and navigation canals, tidal creeks.*

Eastern North Carolina is very green in early summer, and here at the outset of the growing season the grass is cropped close, rolling over the smooth earth like velvet. Black-dirt farms sprout rich vegetation: acres of sod, young soybeans, corn.

We know time is tight to make the 7:45 ferry after encountering a few twists and turns on the way here. (I neglected to print out detailed directions— something I won't forget next time.)

The M/V *Floyd J. Lupton* on the Neuse River (Ferry Division photo)

The Cherry Branch landing can be reached from two directions: from New Bern on the north, or from Jacksonville-Swansboro-Morehead City on the south. We've taken the southerly course, though it's debatable whether this has saved us time. We pick up the blue ferry signs about ten miles after crossing the bridge at Swansboro and again in the community of Havelock, where we make a hard right at the Food Lion, barely taking notice of the new residential subdivisions interspersed with farm and forest.

At the end of the road there's nowhere to go but the ferry queue. As we round the hill there's a good vista overlooking the Neuse River, and a pleasantly shaded picnic area.

But we arrive only in time to see the Neuse *leaving the dock, moving steadily across the river in the direction of an approaching rain shower. It's nearly breezy enough to keep the biting flies away—definitely a good thing. We make the best of it, bringing out the checkered picnic cloth and the sandwiches.*

By the time the M/V Floyd J. Lupton *docks on our side, it's begun to drizzle. There aren't many cars this evening, and we patiently wait for the incoming boat to unload. The first exiting car encounters a bit of a problem, however; its female driver cranks the ignition a few times, but gets only a feeble turn of the engine.*

James Carter works security at Camp Seagull in Minesott Beach and commutes on the ferries.

We watch from the top of the hill as the crew gallantly get behind the Toyota and push. Three of them roll the compact car over the ramp and up the incline in short order. They push it off to the side, where they chat up the driver while she dials her cell phone.

What's the deal with the Toyota? I ask the deckhand as we load.

"Out of gas," he says. "Her boyfriend's going to bring a gas can."

Good thing, I think, since the nearest pump is probably ten miles inland. The unexpected does occur sometimes—stalled engines, overheated radiators—most often, keys locked in cars. The crew have become experts in jimmying locks, but they also know where to call the locksmiths in each ferry town as well.

As the horn sounds and we push off, the rain is really coming down on the deck of the Floyd Lupton. *We pass the time in the lounge with the crew, quizzing them on what it's like to work aboard the ferry, where they live, how they like the work. Many are former or retired Coast Guard; some simply took on the ferry job for a change of pace. Like many of their passengers, they live near one of the landing communities and take the boat across the river whenever it's time to work.*

Nightfall can be one of the most beautiful times to ride the ferries.

The crew handle thirteen-hour shifts on a seven-days-on, seven-days-off rotation. There's a galley for the crew's use, and a television in the passenger lounge. Not to mention that the procession of passengers and vehicles keeps things interesting.

Larry Dean loads 25 to 30 semi trucks a day, many of them big log trucks—there's a lot of logging at Minnesott right now, he says. Seafood trucks, shrimp trucks: anything that runs on the highways can go on the ferry (mobile homes, however, travel a different way). He's carried seven military tanks at a time, a full load for this 40-car ferry (though they call ahead).

Once we land at Minnesott Beach, it's too dark to see much of the surroundings, and rain is pelting down. But even in the dark and downpour we can spot interesting old houses and churches and seafood markets alternating with the cornfields, and this area invites us to come back in sunnier, drier hours.

THE CHERRY BRANCH FERRY landing is situated in the southeastern portion of Craven County, which was named in the early 1700s for the sucessors of one of the original Lords Proprietors of Carolina. The county seat of **New Bern,** a historic city located upstream from the ferry at the confluence of the Trent and Neuse Rivers, is the largest nearby municipality, a 45-minute drive away. **Jacksonville,** in adjoining Onslow County, is about 70 miles from the ferry, but the wilderness of the **Croatan National Forest** lies between and prevents a direct route. The forest covers 157,000 acres of pocosin swamp, a rich habitat for animal and plant life and an out-of-the-way locale for hunting, fishing, and canoeing.

New Bern, settled in 1710 by Swiss and German immigrants and named for Bern, Switzerland, served as North Carolina's colonial and state capital in the eighteenth century. The governor's home, Tryon Palace, has now been restored as a suite of house museums and spectacular seasonal gardens. Flash forward to the beginning of the twentieth century, and the town also became the birthplace of Pepsi-Cola.

New Bern offers several chain hotels, some with attractive waterfront locations. It also has a KOA Kampground and a number of inns and B&Bs. The town is known for

New Bern's historic heritage is evident in the shape of its gentle skyline.

its opportunities for antiques and specialty shopping, as well as a strong tradition of local arts and culture. There's almost always something going on, from a gallery show to a theatre production. For more information, pick up a copy of *New Bern* magazine.

The nearest town to the Cherry Branch ferry landing is **Havelock**, a railroad hamlet from the mid-nineteenth century until the establishment in 1941 of the **Cherry Point Marine Air Station**, now the world's largest U.S. marine air station. Military and civilian personnel employed at the air station constitute an important population of ferry travelers, many commuting across to homes on the opposite side of the river. It's appropriate that the town was named for a military strategist, the Victorian-era British general Sir Henry Havelock.

It's not unusual out here to hear Harriers, C-130s, and other military aircraft soaring far overhead or coming in close for a landing.

Recreational hunting and fishing was popular in the area from the late 1800s into the 1930s—drawing sportsmen like Babe Ruth, Christie Mathewson, and Bud Fisher to its woods and swamps.

There are several chain motels in Have-

lock, though more imaginative accommodations abound on the Crystal Coast beaches a few miles to the south. You'll find groceries at the Food Lion and gas at plenty of convenience stores in town. (Be sure to refuel before heading north on the ferry, as choices on the Pamlico County side are meager.)

Cherry Branch itself might give travelers a bit of uncertainty: one online map search reveals that there are seven such place-names in the state of North Carolina, none of them the site of the ferry. (Yep, that'll confuse the heck out of your vehicle's navigation system.)

The ferry crosses at a bend in the broad estuary of the Neuse River and travels due north to **Minnesott Beach**, in Pamlico County. Most of the county is rural, its low-lying farmlands cultivated in row crops, but its harbors on Pamlico Sound have also become off-the-beaten-path resort destinations. In the early 1900s, the Hardison family developed Minnesott Beach as a waterfront resort. Today, a country club and yacht basin are supplemented by golf and other recreational amenities.

Don't count on readily finding facilities in Minnesott Beach itself—you're in a remote, bucolic area that, although it isn't an island, sometimes feels like one. Many communities, like **Arapahoe** and **Grantsboro**, have grocery and convenience stores, though they're not necessarily open extended hours. **Bayboro**, the Pamlico County seat, has plenty of choices for fast food, gas, banks, and the like, but no overnight lodging.

From the ferry landing, NC 306 proceeds straight northward through drained fields and pine forests, toward the crossroads at **Grantsboro.** A left turn at Grantsboro will take you into New Bern; continuing north will lead to the ferry landing at **Aurora**—but that's another chapter.

Twelve miles east of the ferry landing, along the hem of the peninsula, is **Oriental**, a fishing village and yacht harbor named not for its far-easterly location but for the 1862 wreck of a transport ship whose nameplate washed up nearby a few years later.

Oriental makes the most of its identity, however, with a Chinese-style dragon parade every New Year's Eve and a store offering excellent Asian foods. Be sure to visit Croakertown, on NC Highway 55, and Inland Waterway Provision, at 305 Hodges Street on the harbor.

Although Oriental isn't on the main route to the ferry—or anywhere else, unless you're arriving by water—it's worth a detour to visit. Oriental, with three times as many boats as residents, is a popular stop for intracoastal cruising and the home of major sailing events each fall.

Oriental offers plenty of low-key conveniences. Accommodations are generally B&Bs and guest houses rather than motels—so it's wise to check ahead. In season, rooms stay booked; out of season, they may be closed.

If you're eager for some reading that will get you in the spirit of the sailing life, pick up a copy of Claiborne Young's *Cruising Guide to Coastal North Carolina* or Eddie Jones's humorous *Hard Aground* collections.

For more information
• New Bern/Craven Convention and Visitors Center: www.visitnewbern.com, 1.880.437.5767 or 252.637.9400.
•Pamlico County Chamber of Commerce, 252.745.3008.

Waterfront at Oriental, the "Sailing Capital of North Carolina"

The **Ferries** of North Carolina **53**

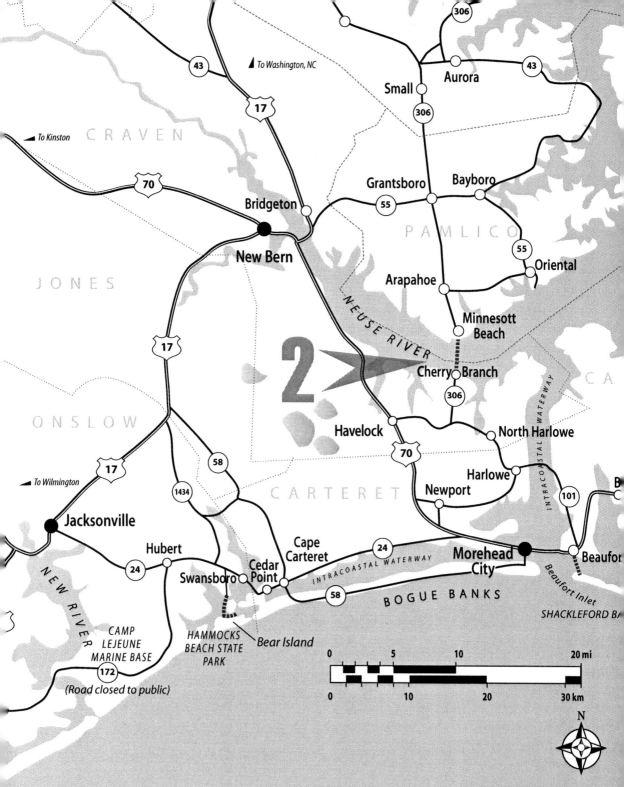

Cherry Branch (southern) landing

Jacksonville, NC, to Cherry Branch ferry landing
From downtown Jacksonville, take NC 24 E / Johnson Blvd. 33 miles through Swansboro, Cape Carteret, and the Croatan National Forest to Hibbs Rd. (NC 1141). Turn left (north) onto Hibbs Road toward Newport and Havelock; proceed 3.2 miles, then turn left onto US 70 W. Follow the four-lane US 70 7.9 miles into Havelock, then bear right onto Cunningham Dr. and turn right onto NC 101 / Fontana Blvd., following the ferry signs. Continue north on NC101 for 5 miles to intersection with NC306 N / Ferry Rd. Turn left and follow NC306 north for 4.8 miles to the ferry landing.
Total est. distance: 50 miles
Total est. time: 1 hour, 15 minutes

Morehead City, NC, to Cherry Branch ferry landing From downtown Morehead City, take US 70 W / Arendell St. 16.7 miles toward Newport and Havelock. Bear right onto Cunningham Drive and turn right onto NC 101 / Fontana Blvd., following the ferry signs. Continue north on NC 101 for 5 miles to intersection with NC306 N / Ferry Rd. Turn left and follow NC306 for 4.8 miles to the ferry landing.
Total est. distance: 27 miles
Total est. time: 45 minutes

From Beaufort, NC, you can take an alternate route via NC 101 north through Harlowe to the intersection with NC 306, then turn right and follow NC306 for 4.8 miles to the ferry landing.
Total est. distance: 23 miles
Total est. time: 40 minutes

New Bern, NC, to Cherry Branch ferry landing
From George St. in downtown New Bern, take the US 70 / US 17/ NC 55 bridge, turning right and merging onto US 70 E toward Havelock. Travel 16.8 miles southeast, through the communities of Riverdale and Pine Grove, to the intersection with NC 101 / Fontana Blvd. Bear left and continue to follow NC 101 south for 5 miles to intersection with NC 306 N / Ferry Rd. Turn left and follow NC306 north for 4.8 miles to the ferry landing.
Total est. distance: 27 miles
Total est. time: 45 minutes

Cedar Island ferry landing to Cherry Branch ferry landing From the ferry landing, take NC 12 for 12 miles, crossing the Monroe Gaskill Bridge, to its end at US 70. Bear right onto US 70 E and follow it for 8.2 miles to the community of Davis. Turn right to stay on US 70 E; follow it for 6.1 miles west to the community of Smyrna. Turn right to stay on US70; follow it for 6.4 miles west through Otway and Bettie, crossing the North River. Once across the bridge, turn right onto Merrimon Road. Proceed north for 2.4 miles, then turn left (west) onto Laurel Road. Follow it for 2.2 miles to the intersection with NC 101; turn right and proceed for 5 miles to intersection with NC306 N / Ferry Rd. Turn right and follow NC306 for 4.8 miles north to the ferry landing.
Total est. distance: 48 miles
Total est. time: 1 hour, 15 minutes

•

Minnesott Beach (northern) landing

New Bern, NC, to Minnesott Beach ferry landing
From George Street in downtown New Bern, take the US 70 / US 17 / NC 55 bridge north and east across the Neuse River (bearing left toward Bridgeton). On the opposite side, follow NC 55 for 10 miles through Reelsboro to the crossroads at Grantsboro. Turn right (south) onto NC 306 / Point Road; proceed 12.5 miles to the Minnesott Beach ferry landing.
Total est. distance: 25 miles
Total est. time: 45 minutes

Aurora ferry landing to Minnesott Beach ferry landing
From the ferry landing, follow NC 306 6.5 miles south, past the PCS Phosphate plant on the right, bypassing the town of Aurora. Turn left onto Main St., Ext. N / NC 306 W fo 0.4 miles, then turn right onto NC 33 . NC 306. Continue for 2.8 miles; bear left to continue on NC 306 through community of Small. Continue on NC 306 south for 23 miles through Grantsboro and Arapahoe, following signs to the Minnesott Beach ferry landing.
Total est. distance: 34 miles
Total est. time: 1 hour, 10 minutes

Aurora– Bayview SCHEDULE

ALL DATES AND TIMES
SUBJECT TO CHANGE
CALL 1.800.BY-FERRY

Map and directions, pp. 62–63

Departs Aurora	Departs Bayview
Year-round schedule	
---	5.30 am
6.15 am	---
---	7.00 am
7.45 am	---
---	8.30 am
9.45 am	---
---	10.30 am
11.15 am	---
---	12.15 pm
12.50 pm	---
---	1.30 pm
2.15 pm	---
---	3.15 pm
4.45 pm	
---	5.30 pm
6.15 pm	---
---	7.00 pm
7.45 pm	---
---	9.15 pm
10.00 pm	---
---	11.00 pm
12.30 am	---

CHAPTER **3** **Aurora–Bayview**

vehicle/passenger ferry

route NC Hwy 306; crosses Pamlico River from outside town of **Aurora** (pop. 580, Beaufort County) to community of Gaylord, outside **Bayview** (Beaufort County)

duration 30 min

distance 2.4 mi

vessels River Class (40 vehicles, 300 passengers): M/V *Gov. Daniel Russell*

fare Free

reservations No

terminal Bayview 252.964.4521 Web www.ncferry.org

shore facilities Aurora: Restrooms, picnic shelters, newspaper rack Bayview: Visitor center with office, Ship's Store, restrooms, water fountain, vending, pay telephone

fact This route is the key means of transportation for workers at the PCS Phosphate plant.

TO GET TO THE AURORA FERRY LANDING *from the historic town of New Bern, as we did this sunny winter afternoon, requires traversing long stretches of swamp and savannah with no towns of any size—where even in daylight it takes a bit of effort to avoid getting lost. (Coming here straight from the Minnesott Beach landing via NC306 is a direct route, but even that involves some easy-to-miss turns.)*

At Grantsboro, we rejoin NC Highway 306, turning north. Jets from the MCAS create a crisscross of contrails that is mirrored by the long ditches cut into the chartreuse fields below.

The twists and turns have taken longer than we bargained for—and in the nine miles remaining till the ferry, we have to slow down. First for the mail truck. Then for three deer grazing on the shoulder. Then for the rail crossing serving the phosphate plant.

The clock in the truck reads 4:44 as I floor the gas

The superstructure of the M/V *Daniel Russell*

again. At least it's set three minutes fast, I remember. Would we make it?

A mile later, we spy the familiar blue sign. We bank to the left to enter the ferry lane. It's a short approach, and a few yards later we zip around the corner and pull up to the ferry entrance.

Marsh creek, Stonewall community, Pamlico County

The boat's still at the dock, her lines intact. But the barrier is down and the gangway's up.

I blow the horn lightly, like clearing my throat for attention, and the deckhand at the stern turns around my way. She motions to her coworker on the other side, who nods, reaches for the switch, and generously lowers the ramp again. We're on!

The attendant waves me over to the far lane, and I roll down my window to thank her for letting us aboard. "Train catch you?" she inquires pleasantly. Regular commuters from the plant must find that a common enough problem.

"No, just cutting it close," I admit.

In the lounge, the only other occupant is a young man talking on a cell phone. When he finishes his call, he tells me that he's putting in several days of community service, part of his penalty for a recent DUI.

"I done made nineteen trips on this boat today," he tells me. His chores have been menial—he's been assigned to clean the boat, a job that involves working with the crew scrubbing down the engine room below. Although he lives more than an hour away and isn't keen to thumb a ride all the way to the landing, the work hasn't been all that bad—a few more stints and he'll be done.

When we reach port on the Bayview side I thank the ferrywoman again. Since we're the last vehicle off, I take a moment to tell her about the book I'm writing. I ask if she knows of a good place to spend the night in the area.

"Oh, sure," she says. "The River Forest Manor, over in Belhaven." I envision a single-story cinder-block strip with log trucks parked in the lot, but we jot it down anyway. In the meantime, the deckhand, B. S. Purifoy according to her badge, is so taken with my project she motions to her colleagues, B. T. Quidley and B. P. "Cap'n Ben" Wilkins—all of whom have finished their shifts for the day and are signing off. They're eager to get to dinner, until they realize they have a ready audience for their ample store of tales.

Purifoy says Cap'n Ben, who's been with the ferry service for more than thirty years, knows everything.

"He's 'Ben' Laden," quips Quidley. Oh, and did I know that the ferries have been featured

in movies? Quidley asks me. (The old Sea Level *played a role in Robert DeNiro's 1991 remake of* Cape Fear *as well as 1997's* The Jackal *and 1998's* The Wedding).*

When the original Sea Level *was retired in 200, Cap'n Ben and his crew mounted her license case here in the Bayview visitor center. It now houses a knot board made by the crew, featuring difficult and unusual patterns alongside ordinary slipknots and clove hitches, and an a fascinating array of carved miniatures.*

We thank the three B's for the impromptu tour and promise to come back, but leave them to their well-deserved time off. Now, to find that River Forest Manor place before dark . . . .

name from the newspaper once published there, called *Aurora Borealis.* Today, phosphate mining plays an important part in the local economy. The Aurora Fossil Museum— a storefront on Main Street—presents the geological history of eastern North Carolina.

Captain Ben Wilkins shows the knot board he and his colleagues mounted on the license board from the old *Sea Level.*

TO REACH THE AURORA LANDING, keep a sharp eye at the twists and turns of NC 33 and 306. Navigating the narrow roads after dark, or in a downpour, is a challenge— the two-lane road is illuminated only at infrequent street crossings with street lamps hung over the center line.

The road to the ferry turns off before **Aurora**, the town it's named for—originally a free black settlement that in turn took its

Lodgings and dining opportunities in Aurora are few, but you will find a Piggly Wiggly and a Dollar General, as well as a convenience store.

Travelers taking the ferries might find **Washington, N.C.,** with its B&Bs, chain motels, and restaurants, their logical jumping-off place and **Bath**, the state's oldest town, an interesting diversion along NC Highway 92/99, one of the state's designated Scenic Byways. (If you're into pirate lore, you might want to learn more about Bath's connec-

The **Ferries** of North Carolina **59**

The River Forest Manor, Belhaven

tion with Edward Teach, the infamous Blackbeard, who lived here for a time in the 1700s.)

On the northern side of the Pamlico River from Aurora the ferry lands at a spot in the road known as **Gaylord**, though there are no facilities here other than the ferry office, and the nearby community named **Bayview** offers no public services. A number of popular summer camps are located along the soundfront. To the northwest lie **Bath, Goose Creek State Park,** and **Washington**; to the northeast, the harbor community of Belhaven.

Belhaven, situated where Pantego Creek empties into the tidal Pungo River, is one of this region's unexpected delights. Close enough to either the Bayview or Swan Quarter ferries to provide a comfortable night's rest before an early morning departure, it's one of those places that might make you decide to rebook your boat ride and stay a little longer.

We dial the Manor on the cell, not just a little surprised to find service out here, and reach a friendly voice that assures us there's a room for tonight, even though it's still quite out of season. Yes, the woman says, come on.

The short drive into Belhaven takes us through a primitive landscape of marsh creeks, straight tall trees branchless to the very top of the canopy, water that fraternizes easily with the neat, flat, grassy banks. Watercourses and the earth interlock like pieces of a jigsaw puzzle.

Toward the eastern end of Belhaven's Main Street, we're in for a surprise. The grand white columns of the River Forest Manor dominate a waterfront lawn under towering pines.

The affable older woman we'd talked with on the phone, Lee Roberts (not her real name, she tells me) came here to Belhaven in 1945 to marry. "If I hadn't been the kind of personality I am now," she says, "I would have packed up and gone back to New York on the first bus."

But she stayed. She saw Belhaven in its boom times, when there was lots of bustling commerce in timber and railroads and fisheries. She saw the last downtown retail establishment, a Rose's department store, close its doors in 1984, and when that happened, "Everybody left. Everything left."

Hurricane Fran brought further desolation in 1996, with a devastating storm surge that damaged many homes and businesses. But the mayor was determined not to give up on the beleaguered town. His aggressive pursuit of federal emergency funding, and a concerted plan to elevate and rebuild many of Belhaven's characteristic turn-of-the-century homes, paid off.

Restoration was soon followed by new construction, and today Belhaven is a picturesque harbor community where retirement living, boating on the Intracoastal, and tourism thrive alongside a viable, though less visible, fishing industry.

Facilities and provisions

In Belhaven you'll find a choice of restaurants (seafood, of course), drugstore and convenience shopping, marina supplies, and gift and clothing boutiques. The town puts on an annual bluegrass and hot-air balloon festival. During regular business hours, Belhaven is s a good place to restock and refuel before the passage to Ocracoke.

The town also boasts several B&Bs, including the Thistle Dew and Thomasina's. If it's a budget motel, a hunting cabin, an RV resort, or a camping spot you're looking for, Beaufort and Hyde Counties offer those as well—but since everything in this part of the state is off the beaten path, be sure to do your research before leaving home and your driving before dark.

If the River Forest Manor lacks the upscale touches of the luxury chain hotels (you won't find a built-in hair dryer or high-speed Internet connection here), it more than makes up for it in period charm. Like an eccentric great-aunt, it presents a character and demeanor part Victorian high-toned elegance, part Southern good manners, part forgivable quirks. Its dark wood furnishings, high ceilings, and patterned wallpapers speak

of an era when this was the grand home of an executive with the Norfolk & Southern Railroad and the J. L. Roper Lumber Company.

Built in 1904, the elaborate mansion remained a private home until 1947, when it was purchased by Axson Smith, a hotelier whose résumé listed experience with the Drake and Palmer House of Chicago. Development of a full-service marina, a swimming pool, and tennis courts, as well as a fine-dining restaurant and a lounge, transformed the huge home into a resort hotel.

In the post-Fran years, management has gone for a bed-and-breakfast approach. The restaurant is open in season; but even in the off-season the lounge provides spirits and snacks as well as a crackling fire. A spacious elevated deck overlooks the Pungo River. There's an upright piano in the lounge, and there are organs in the lounge and in the grand foyer.

In this laid-back neck of eastern North Carolina, you're in prime territory for boating, fishing, birding, and hunting. So take it easy and enjoy the scenery.

For more information
• Historic Bath Visitors Center, 252.923.3971
• Belhaven Community Chamber of Commerce, 252.943.3770

The **Ferries** of North Carolina

Aurora landing (south bank of Pamlico River)

Minnesott Beach ferry to Aurora ferry

From the ferry landing, follow NC 306 north 23 miles through the communities of Arapahoe and Grantsboro to the crossroads of Small; just past Small bear right to continue on NC 33/ NC 306. Continue for 2.8 miles. At ferry sign ("Ferry 7 Miles") bear left onto Main St. Ext. N / NC 306 E for 0.4 miles, then turn left onto NC 306 / Hickory Point Rd., bypassing the town of Aurora. Continue 6.5 miles past the PCS Phosphate plant on left; follow the ferry signs and turn left at Aurora landing.
Total est. distance: 34 miles
Total est. time: 50 minutes

Washington, NC, to Aurora ferry landing

From downtown Washington, take US 17 S / N. Bridge St. across the Pamlico River. Continue to follow US 17 south for 3.5 miles to the intersection with NC 33 in the town of Chocowinity. Turn left onto NC 33 and follow it for 21.4 miles through the communities of Rover, Coxs Crossroads, and Edward. Just past Edward, NC 33 will intersect with NC 306; turn left to stay on NC 33 / NC 306.

Continue for 3 miles. Bear left onto Main St. Ext. N / NC 306 E for 0.4 miles, then turn left onto NC 306 / Hickory Point Rd., bypassing the town of Aurora. Continue 6.5 miles past the PCS Phosphate plant on left; follow the ferry signs and turn left at Aurora landing.
Total est. distance: 35 miles
Total est. time: 55 minutes

Bayview landing (north bank of Pamlico River)

Washington, NC, to Bayview ferry landing

From downtown Washington, take US 264 E / NC 92 / W. R. "Bill" Roberson Jr. Hwy. / W. 5th St. Continue on NC92 9.5 miles to the community of Midway; bear right to continue on NC 92 E, designated an NC Scenic Byway. (An alternate route continues on US 264 about 10 miles to the community to Yeatesville, where a right turn on Yeatesville Rd. /Burbage Rd. and left turn on NC 99 will also lead to the ferry.) Follow NC 92 east through historic Bath 11.1 miles to the community of Gaylord; turn right onto NC 306, following the ferry signs 1/4 mile to the Bayview landing.
Total est. distance: 21 miles
Total est. time: 35 minutes

Belhaven, NC, to Bayview ferry landing

From downtown Belhaven, take NC 99 W across the bridge toward Smithtown and Sidney. Continue 11.4 miles west until NC 99 becomes NC 92 in the community of Gaylord. Turn left onto NC 306 and proceed 1/4 mile to the ferry landing.
Total est. distance: 12 miles
Total est. time: 20 minutes

PCS Phosphate mine, Aurora

Cedar Island– Ocracoke SCHEDULE

ALL DATES AND TIMES
SUBJECT TO CHANGE
CALL 1.800.BY-FERRY

Map and directions, pp. 72–73

Off Season

Departs Cedar Island	Departs Ocracoke
JAN 1, 2007 – APRIL 2, 2007 NOV 6, 2007 – MAR 17, 2008	
7.00 am	7.00 am
10.00 am	10.00 am
1.00 pm	1.00 pm
4.30 pm	4.00 pm

Shoulder Season

Departs Cedar Island	Departs Ocracoke
APRIL 3 — MAY 14, 2007 OCT 9 – NOV 5, 2007	
7.00 am	7.00 am
9.30 am	9.30 am
12.00 noon	12.00 noon
3.00 pm	3.00 pm
6.00 pm	6.00 pm
8:30 pm	8.30 pm

High Season

Departs Cedar Island	Departs Ocracoke
MAY 15 – OCT 8, 2007	
7.00 am	7.00 am
8.15 am	---
9.30 am	9.30 am
---	10.45 am
12.00 noon	12.00 noon
1.15 pm	---
3.00 pm	3.00 pm
	4.15 pm
6.00 pm	6.00 pm
8.30 pm	8.30 pm

The *Pamlico* in port, Cedar Island

CHAPTER 4

Cedar Island–Ocracoke

vehicle/passenger ferry

route NC Hwy. 12; crosses southwestern end of Pamlico Sound from **Cedar Island** (pop. 350, Carteret County) to village of **Ocracoke** (pop. 750, Hyde County) on Ocracoke Island

duration 2 hrs 25 min

distance 23.5 mi

vessels Sound class (50 vehicles, 300 passengers): M/V *Carteret*, M/V *Cedar Island*, M/V *Pamlico*, M/V *Silver Lake*

fare One way
Pedestrian $1.00
Bicycle rider $3.00
Motorcycle $10.00
Vehicle and/or combination less than 20' $15.00
Vehicle and/or combination 20' up to 40' $30.00
Vehicle and/or combination over 40' up to 65' $45.00

reservations and terminal information
Cedar Island 3619 Cedar Island Rd., Cedar Island NC 28520-9634
1.800.856.0343
252.225.3551
Ocracoke
1.800.345.1665
252.928.3841
Web www.ncferry.org

shore facilities Cedar Island: Visitor center with offices, Ship's Store, restrooms, vending, coffee, pay telephones
Ocracoke: Visitor center with with offices, lounge, Ship's Store, restrooms, vending, coffee, pay telephones

fact The Cedar Island to Ocracoke ferry route features the largest vessels in the state's fleet, at 220' in length.

OLD CEDAR ISLAND ROAD LEADS *out of Atlantic, N.C., back to route 12, where it comes out just half a mile ahead of the Monroe Gaskill bridge over Thorofare Bay. I've expectantly driven this route on many occasions, and the sun is starting to shine invitingly on the rainbow arc of the bridge. But this time my hopes sink a bit when I encounter a three-rung orange-striped barrier squarely in our lane. Road Closed Due to High Water. No mistaking that message.*

Must not've been moved back since the rain stopped, I tell myself (really, I'm justifying)—but after all, the barrier isn't blocking the other lane. I drive around. If we encounter high water, surely we'll see it in plenty of time, on the flat, straight expanse of road on the other side of the bridge. And besides, if we saw traffic coming from the other way, we'd know they hadn't had a problem getting through.

If I had realized how little room the narrow lanes afford for turning around, I might not have ventured forward. From the top of the bridge, what is usually a broad sea of grass on either side of the highway appears instead to be one endless, smooth lake with a thin strip of gray paper ribbon floating on its surface. I creep ahead more slowly than I have planned.

Piles of dead cordgrass have blown against the sides of the road in places, helping mark the edge of the lane. Chunks of foam skid across the asphalt in the wind. Birds, always numerous in this region, are absent. At no place does water

Road Closed Due to High Water: Believe it!

intrepid year-round residents of this settlement routinely deal with worse.

Encountering one other flooded section much like the first, I'm grateful to pull up into the ferry line and find not only a few other signs of vehicles and drivers, but the ferry-boat still in port. Ten minutes to spare, and it doesn't appear there's even a huge rush to board. We should've wondered about that.

cross the road entirely, to my relief—but no car approaches us from the east, either, until we are fully past the miles of marsh and safely on the higher ground where houses and churches cluster.

It's in the first of these two villages, where the road makes a sharp bend, that I see how serious the warning has been. A dip in the road, perhaps fifty yards across, is below water, where the tidal creek on one side has risen to join forces with the boat slip on the other. Reason says the water couldn't possibly be very deep over the road—but how to tell where road gives way to shoulder or creek bank?

The slanting afternoon sun shines through the clear brackish water as I inch into it. I follow the yellow stripe, fully a foot beneath the creek, until it rises and becomes dry road surface once again. Fording the stream at night, or with the tide moving more swiftly, would not have been wise—though I have to imagine that the

ON THIS SATURDAY NIGHT IN April, things are hopping at the Driftwood Motel restaurant—the ferry's not running because of the high water on the **Cedar Island** side of Highway 12.

People arrive seeking shelter, coming in from the spring storm like it's Nantucket in November in a Melville novel. By the time the clam chowder has arrived, steaming and delicious, we feel as snug as in a New England inn before a roaring hearth—though it's just a one-story cinder-block structure beside the dunes.

The motel is glad to feed people—locals and tourists alike—and put folks up for the night at a reasonable rate. And that's a good thing, since it's the only permanent hostelry on the island—and situated more than twenty miles from the nearest late-hours gas station.

The cozy dining room features rope-trimmed porthole windows, wood-paneled interior, and very good homestyle seafood. The staff are friendly and helpful.

Manager June Fulcher's mother-in-law opened a grill and fishing pier at this far end of the island in the late 1950s—back when the ferry ran from Atlantic instead of here—and then in the 1960s built nine motel units and sold the rights to the pier to the ferry folks. The Fulchers promptly added fourteen more units, and then built another wing in the 1970s. The motel now operates year-round, though the restaurant is open full-time just nine months. During the off-season, they'll still open up for breakfast, or on weekends and holidays when people come out to hunt and fish.

There's a certain kind of tourist who likes the unspoiled, undeveloped beaches of Cedar Island, June Fulcher explains, the kind of visitor who takes pleasure in the quiet, the remoteness, in camping by the bay or riding horseback on the strand. "We see all kinds of really, really nice people through here," she assures me.

The **Cedar Island National Wildlife Refuge** was established in 1964, the same year the ferry landing was moved here.

In autumn and winter, many thousands of waterfowl, including tundra swans, migrate to the marsh. The wildlife refuge is open to the public free of charge, but there are no improved facilities. The nearest gas stations are inland at Davis and Atlantic; the nearest supermarket, besides the Red & White in

Cedar Island National Wildlife Refuge

Atlantic and the convenience stores situated at major crossroads, is on the outskirts of Beaufort. The Driftwood, however, offers camping, swimming, boating, windsurfing and kiteboarding, and even beachfront horseback riding.

Over time the Driftwood Restaurant began to build a reputation for its fresh local seafood, and before long ferry riders were coming early to have dinner before boarding. Occsionally, of course, they arrive too late and miss their intended ferry. Mrs. Fulcher is more than happy to help them make the best of the situation with a warm meal or, if needed, a warm bed for the night.

And that's the case for us this Saturday. We turn in for a good night's sleep, showered and well fed, between clean sheets. I dream myself adrift on a shallow bay, floating on a raft that glides across the vast sea of grass, shifts oceanward and back on the waves, unhindered, unpiloted, unconcerned.

•

We wake at dark the next morning and go out to check the ferry schedule. Breakfast is already spread on the restaurant's

At the Cedar Island lading, the Driftwood Motel and Restaurant provides a welcome haven.

buffet—muffins and Danish pastries, coffee and juice. We pack up and get ready just in case, wolf down a quick bite.

The sun's just beginning to come up when the ticket clerk pops in and says it looks like the weather has finally eased up. "Ferry's goin'!" he announces to the din-ing room before heading out to the motel to knock on the door of the guest who wanted to be roused in case the first run was a go. Everyone in the place springs swiftly into action.

I drive the Passport into a steadily swelling queue. The sun rises bright and clear through a few broken clouds, the boat is loaded, the horn sounds, and we're on our way.

At the Pony Island Restaurant on Ocracoke later in the day, we learn the full scoop about the storm: a nor'easter had blown in on Wednesday night, bringing 60-mile-an-hour winds to the entire Down East area and the Outer Banks. It's blown for three days, during which time officals closed the bridge at Manteo and held the ferries in port. As the wind picked up, the smaller ferry—the *Hyde*—could sail safely, but the large boats with their taller superstructures couldn't make the run. The Ocracokers and ferry crewmen alike tell us that sort of a shutdown is a rarity.

The waitress, in a waist-length brunette braid, tells us about one of her hapless customers, a fellow who walked onto the Cedar Island ferry on Wednesday afternoon for a day trip, then got to Ocracoke only to find the ferry wasn't making the return run. He had $15 in cash, wore nothing thicker than a T-shirt, and brought no spare clothes. He didn't get back to the mainland till Sunday morning.

Some of the restuarant's patrons had driven down from Viriginia and had been captive on Ocracoke the whole time. All the tourists agreed on one thing: they hadn't seen any weather warning worse than "windy" and didn't know to stay home and postpone their Outer Banks trip till another day.

•

On the return trip to Cedar Island this afternoon, the wind has calmed so much that occasionally the flags go slack, the anemometer spins lazily, the gulls hold their perches on the davits and instrument masts without effort. On the far Southern horizon we can see the narrow white needle of the lighthouse at Cape Lookout.

The captain reverses the propellers in the turning basin to bring the stern around, cuts the engine, gives it a little throttle accompanied by a gust of diesel smoke, and maneuvers toward its rendezvous with the dock. He lets it drift, lets the current take it into the pilings, nudge it alongside the rubber bumpers.

Once more, we've returned. For us, it's the road home. For the ferrymen, just another relay, touching base before they turn and do it again.

•

FOR TRAVELERS HEADED FROM points south to North Carolina's Outer Banks, the ferry to **Ocracoke Island** is their most sensible route. From Cedar Island or Swan Quarter, the boats cross Pamlico Sound to dock at the village of Ocracoke, on the south-

The Ocracoke Lighthouse, built in 1823, is the oldest in operation on America's East Coast.

ern tip of the island, a narrow, twelve-mile strip of sand dunes with no bridge acesss at either end. (The alternative ways to get to any of the Outer Banks are by bridge at Manteo, on the northern end, or by private boat or small plane.)

Lest that sound too desolate, Ocracoke is a haven of slow-paced beach culture, casual comfort, and natural and historic wonders.

A port since 1715, Ocracoke was once

home to both pirates and ship's pilots. The present lighthouse, built in 1823, is the oldest still in operation on the eastern U.S. coast.

Facilities, activities, and provisions. The island features 16 miles of unspoiled beaches as part of the **Cape Hatteras National Seashore,** so all commercial activity is concentrated in the village, close to the Silver Lake harbor. Dining choices are many and intriguing; shopping and galleries are nestled along tree-shaded lanes; water sports and rentals are readily available; and lodgings range from elegant inns to cozy B&Bs to resort homes. There are no chain motels, though several independent establishments, such as the Silver Lake Inn, the Pony Island Motel, and Blackbeard's Lodge, are open year-round, with nightly rates.

Rental ac-

comodations are concentrated near the harbor, oceanside, marshside, or soundside at the southern end. A National Park Service campground is located three miles north of the village; facilities are limited, but the campground is popular, so reservations are recommended. Several private campgrounds are located near the village. There are no lodgings or commercial facilities located near the northern ferry terminal.

Food, supplies, and gas are available at the Ocracoke Variety Store and the Community Store of Ocracoke, which also has an ATM. The East Carolina Bank is located in the village across from the Pony Island Restaurant. The post office and the ABC store are on NC 12 next to the Ocracoke Variety Store. Many specialty

When you're traveling to the Outer Banks beaches, it's smart to be prepared.

and gift stores are open seasonally during business hours.

Guided walking tours introduce visitors to the **highlights of the village**, including the National Park Visitors Center, the British Cemetery, Silver Lake, and historic churches. Away from the village, don't miss the nature trail and the pasture where the island's famous ponies—descendants of a centuries-old mystery—are kept.

For pedestrian access to the **beaches,** park in public lots or alongside Highway 12 and cross over the dunes. There are no lifeguards on Ocracoke's beaches; currents may be strong and waves may be high, so take caution in swimming, wading, or surfing. For pets on the beach, leash laws vary among municipalities along the Outer Banks—you'll need to check local ordinances.

Vehicles with four-wheel drive are allowed on the beach at designated locations. Use marked access roads and follow all park regulations; the standard speed limit on the strand is 25 mph. (For more about beach driving, see chapter 13.)

Ocracoke Island is accessible year-round except in severe weather. Its climate appeals to different people in different seasons. High wind and water on rare occasion make roads impassable during the winter months; hurricanes sometimes threaten the islands

from June 1 to November 1. If you're unsure about weather conditions, call ahead to the visitor center.

There's lots of good reading about Ocracoke, from children's books to romances to straight history. But one of the most delicious ways to get to know the island

Coast Guard station beside ferry dock, Ocracoke

is Charles Harry Whedbee's *Outer Banks Mysteries and Other Seaside Stories* (and anything else by Judge Whedbee).

For more information
• Outer Banks Chamber of Commerce, Kill Devil Hills, 252.441.8144
• Ocracoke Visitors Center, 252.928.6711
• National Park Service, Ocracoke, 252.938.4531

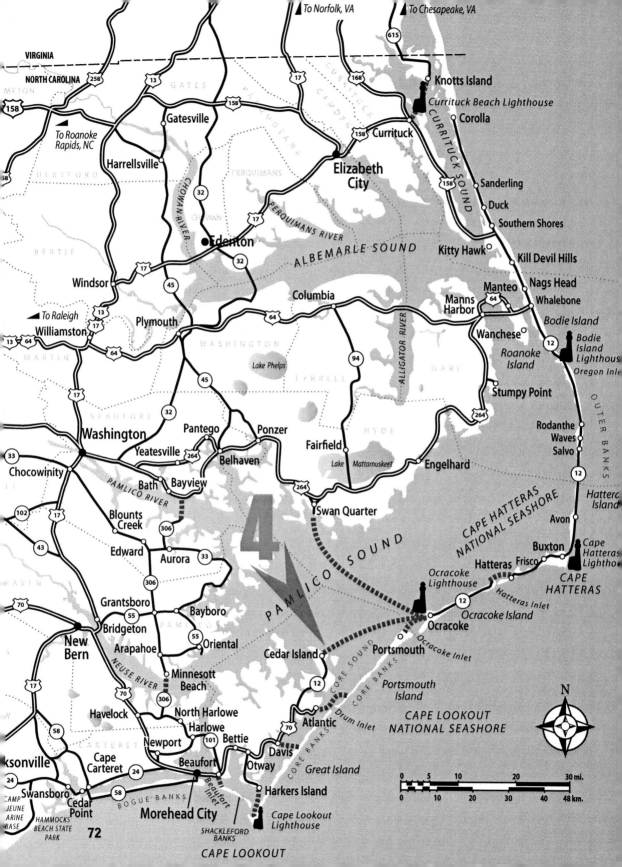

Cedar Island–Ocracoke GETTING THERE

Morehead City, NC, to Cedar Island ferry landing
From Arendell St. in downtown Morehead City, take US 70 E east across the bridges to Beaufort, about 5 miles. In downtown Beaufort, stay on US 70 / Cedar St. for 8 blocks; turn left (north) at Live Oak St. and stay US 70 for 5.2 miles. Follow US 70 E for 5.2 miles to the community of North River Center. (Look for East Carteret High School and the Cape Lookout sign.) Turn right (east) to stay on US 70 / Merrimon Rd., crossing the bridge over the North River and continuing 6.4 miles through the communities of Bettie and Otway to the stop sign in the community of Smyrna. Turn left to stay on US 70, following the ferry signs. Proceed 6.1 miles through the community of Davis; turn left to stay on US 70. Follow US 70 for 8.2 miles to the intersection with NC 12 (here US 70 will continue east to Sea Level and Atlantic). Bear right on NC 12; proceed 12 miles east, across the Monroe Gaskill bridge and the Cedar Island National Wildlife Refuge, to the ferry landing.
Total est. distance: 42 miles
Total est. time: 1 hour 10 minutes, under ideal traffic and weather conditions

Ocracoke ferry landing (N) to Ocracoke ferry landing (S)
From the ferry travel NC 12 southwest for 19.3 miles. At the village of Ocracoke, turn right and proceed 0.7 miles around Silver Lake to the Ocracoke ferry landing.
Total est. distance: 20 miles
Total est. time: 35–40 minutes, depending on traffic

PRAYER OF DEDICATION FOR THE M/V *CEDAR ISLAND*

O, God of all creation, grant thy blessing upon this vessel,
that thy divine providence will protect her
and keep safe from harm this ship, her crew and her passengers.
Let now one of your guardian angels be the constant companion of this ship and her cargo.
May no storm come so quickly that her safety will ever be in doubt,
may no darkness ever confound her watch,
and may the calmness of a morning and the beauty of a sunset
always remind us of your watchful eye.
In the name of the Father, Son and Holy Spirit we now dedicate this vessel
to the service of mankind and for the good of the people of this great state. Amen.

Dedication Ceremony
May 22, 1995

(Printed on a plaque in the ferry's passenger lounge)

Swan Quarter– Ocracoke SCHEDULE

ALL DATES AND TIMES
SUBJECT TO CHANGE
CALL 1.800.BY-FERRY

Map and directions, pp. 80–81

Off Season		High Season	
Departs Swan Quarter	Departs Ocracoke	Departs Swan Quarter	Departs Ocracoke
JAN 1 – MAY 2, 2007 SEPT 4, 2007 – MAY 19, 2008		MAY 22 – SEPT 3, 2007	
---	6.30 am	7.00 am	6.30 am
9.30 pm	---	9.30 am	10.00 am
---	12.30 pm	1.00 pm	12.30 pm
4.00 pm	---	4.00 pm	4.00 pm

A pair of wood ducks
paddle through cedar-
lined marsh

CHAPTER **5** # Swan Quarter–Ocracoke

vehicle/passenger ferry

route NC Hwy. 45; crosses center of Pamlico Sound from **Swan Quarter** (pop. 958, Hyde County) to village of **Ocracoke** (pop. 750, Hyde County) on Ocracoke Island

duration 2 hrs 30 min

distance 27 mi

vessels Sound class (35 vehicles, 300 passengers): M/V *Gov. Edward Hyde*

fare One way
Pedestrian $1.00
Bicycle Rider $3.00
Motorcycles $10.00
Vehicle and/or combination less than 20' $15.00
Vehicle and/or combination 20' up to 40' $30.00
Vehicle and/or combination over 40' up to 65' $45.00

reservations and terminal information
Swan Quarter 1.800.773.1094
252.926.1111
Ocracoke
1.800.345.1665
252.928.3841
Web www.ncferry.org

shore facilities Swan Quarter: Visitor center with office, small Ship's Store, restrooms, vending, coffee, pay phone
Ocracoke: Visitor center with with offices, lounge, Ship's Store, restrooms, vending, coffee, pay telephones

fact The Swan Quarter ferry route is the longest in the North Carolina state system.

ON PAMLICO SOUND, A LONELY *fishing boat lowers crab pots. A few birds fly overhead, crossing a mixed sky of clouds and sun.*

Under the shaded part of the M/V Gov. Edward Hyde's *vehicle deck, a vacationing family has staked out a relaxing spot in the bed of their pickup. The Bowens—Stacey and Kris, and their children Eliza and Nathaniel and dog Derby—are ready for a summer weekend on the Outer Banks.*

Though they live in nearby Belhaven on the mainland, they definitely feel the ferry ride to the islands is special: "You just don't find this everywhere," says Kris. When husband Stacey was in New York not long ago and took the Long Island Ferry, it cost him $55. The $15 crossing to the Outer Banks, he feels, is a bargain—"you'd pay anything" for the OBX experience.

Like the Bowens, we have come to understand

Historic courthouse, Swan Quarter

something of what makes this part of the world so special. The night before, fighting fatigue and intermittent rain as we drove the narrow highway in search of our campground, we seriously doubted our wisdom in pitching a tent at midnight when the ferry would depart at seven in the morning.

The only tenters at the Osprey Nest Campground on the shores of Lake Mattamuskeet

around their flared trunks. Tree frogs began to tune their music to the gentle, rhythmic splash of ripples against the shoreline, while spent thunder echoed in the distance across the sound. Flashes of lightning still played through the air on the far side of the lake, intermittently outlining the shapes of night-flying geese in momentary brilliance. Who could resist sleeping in the open air, beneath such magic?

Crab pots, Swan Quarter docks

After deep sleep, the morning is still dark. A smattering of raindrops threaten but are gone by the time we have the coffee brewed on the propane burner and our egg biscuits warmed in the frying pan. We pay up, slipping our ten-dollar bill into the hosts' mailbox, and hit the road as the sun begins to peek over the wild fields of Hyde County.

(a.k.a. Lake Mattamosquito when I was a kid), we cut the lights, decided not to wake the owners, and thought seriously of just rearranging the gear and spreading the sleeping bags in the cargo area of the Passport.

But the rain let up momentarily, and as we stepped out of the truck we could see the huge, haloed moon suspended over the tops of the cypress trees, the ghostly shores of the lake lapping

TO GET TO THE SWAN QUARTER ferry landing requires driving twisting, two-lane roads with several intersections to navigate—though the reward is worth it. There are no direct routes to Land's End: you must watch closely for the blue ferry signs.

Outside Belhaven, a short spur of highway connects Pamlico Street with US 264, a scenic road quieter than busy US 64, the major artery from inland cities to Nag's Head. Along this stretch of eastern Beaufort County the farmlands are ditched and drained. Dilapidated farmhouses sit back from the road. Just over the Hyde County line at **Ponzer,** "The Store" isn't open—not at this early hour, maybe never.

Bearing right, you stay on 264, which becomes a mere strip between wide ditches, stumps of damaged trees along the margins amputated for motorists' safety. Crude stiles offer occasional access to the woods on the opposite banks; gravesites occupy cleared patches of high ground.

A tall bridge carries you over the Intracoastal Waterway at the Pungo River–Alligator River Canal. A sign proclaims Hyde County "The Road Less Traveled," an understatement most days. At the fishery hamlet of **Rose Bay** flashes a lone traffic light, the only one in the entire county.

At the sign for Swan Quarter, bear right on NC45E at the sign; from there it's a short way to the center of town. A convenience store and a Cash Points ATM high up on piers constitute Swan Quarter's commercial core. Pat's, at the corner by the courthouse, pumps gas if you're here during the right hours.

Swan Quarter is a smallish settlement, its houses mostly raised up out of the reach of flooding, its government buildings clustered tightly together on the miniscule town square. It's the seat of Hyde County, and its courthouse, built about 1854, is listed on the National Register of Historic Places. For a quirky twist of local history, visit "The

The historic Lake Mattamuskeet Lodge, once a pumping station for an ambitious reclamation project, is now a landmark within the wildlife refuge.

Church Moved by the Hand of God" in the storm and flood of 1876.

At the first stop sign, turn left on Main Street, beside the red-brick courthouse, then immediately right again. Several yards along, the ferry sign directs you to turn right for the landing.

If you're wondering what else there is to Swan Quarter—well, back at the stop sign turn right and you'll come to the docks and seafood packing companies. Or if you continued straight instead of turning on Oyster Creek Street you'd eventually come to the shores of Lake Mattamuskeet. That's about it. Out on the highway there's a small grocery store and a hardware store. Don't count on purchasing food, gas, or other provisions except during business hours—and don't count

The M/V *Gov. Edward Hyde* in port

cities like Raleigh and Greenville.

The *Gov. Edward Hyde,* based here, makes two crossings a day year-round; in the summer season, from late May through September, it is joined by the *Silver Lake* and the *Pamlico,* which come over from Ocracoke and rotate on runs from Cedar Island.

on much even then. If you need to spend the night, better have a fold-down seatback in your car.

At the ferry landing there's a cinder-block ferry office with restrooms, vending machines, and a small but comfortable seating area and Ship's Store with memorabilia, information, and brochures.

Gladys Brooks has been with the ferry service since it began here in 1977. The route was added, she says, to allow residents of Ocracoke Island, also in Hyde County, an efficient way to travel to the county seat. As a *Washington (N.C.) Daily News* article put it, "Until June 25 [1977, when service was instituted], anybody living on Ocracoke who wanted to take care of business at the county courthouse had a journey in his future, a 300-mile round trip, to be precise." As for traffic going the other way, Swan Quarter offers the closest route to the island from

Quite aside from the ferry, the landscape, wildlife, and history of mainland **Hyde County** are worthy of exploration. Whether you're traveling to the ferry from points north with a little extra time, or staying overnight before a morning departure, this distant part of the peninsula is unlike any other part of the state.

On the map you can picture Hyde County as an open oyster shell holding **Lake Mattamuskeet** in the middle of its shallow center. On the southern side of the lake, Highway 94 turns left off 264 at Soule Cemetery, where there is a school and a general store, which serves the visiting hunters and fishers as well as the miners and farmers and a few others who make their living here. The manmade causeway over Lake Mattamuskeet passes under silver branches, past ponds where in winter hundreds of white swans rest. Further along more swans, tails upturned as they feed on the shallow bottom, dot the lake surface like a flotilla of miniature sailboats tacking into the wind. In a myrtle bush beside an orange field of sedge, a bright cardinal stands out like a red pennant.

A gravel road turns off toward the **Mattamuskeet National Wildlife Refuge** headquarters, which occupies the site of a power plant, a lodge, and other buildings once designed as a planned farming community on dredged-and-filled land. The experiment proved too costly, and the 18-by-6-mile pocosin lake and its network of canals has now been preserved by the federal government as a haven for migratory birds. (Although the Lodge is no longer in operation, primitive camping is allowed within the refuge.)

Several private campgrounds in the county offer facilities from tent and trailer sites to cabins, and many hunting lodges are open to the public. The Mattamuskeet Inn in **Fairfield** is rustic but comfortable for outdoors types. With its charming white Victorian buildings, Fairfield is an interesting National Register Historic District.

Past Fairfield, Highway 94 crosses the Intracoastal Waterway canal and continues north toward the town of Columbia, on Albemarle Sound in Tyrrell County; or, returning

A motley crew of Tyrrell County–bound tourists ham it up for the camera while waiting for the old Alligator River ferry, 1952. (Courtesy North Carolina State Archives)

to Rose Bay, NC 45, the old Turnpike Road, goes to Plymouth.

Engelhard, on US 264 some 23 miles east of Swan Quarter, offers homestyle dining popular with the locals, as well as the legendary Jennette's Lodge and a grocery store.

For more information
For more on Ocracoke and Ocracoke Island, see chapter 4.
• Greater Hyde County Chamber of Commerce, www.hydecounty.org, 1.888.493.3826 or 252.926.9171

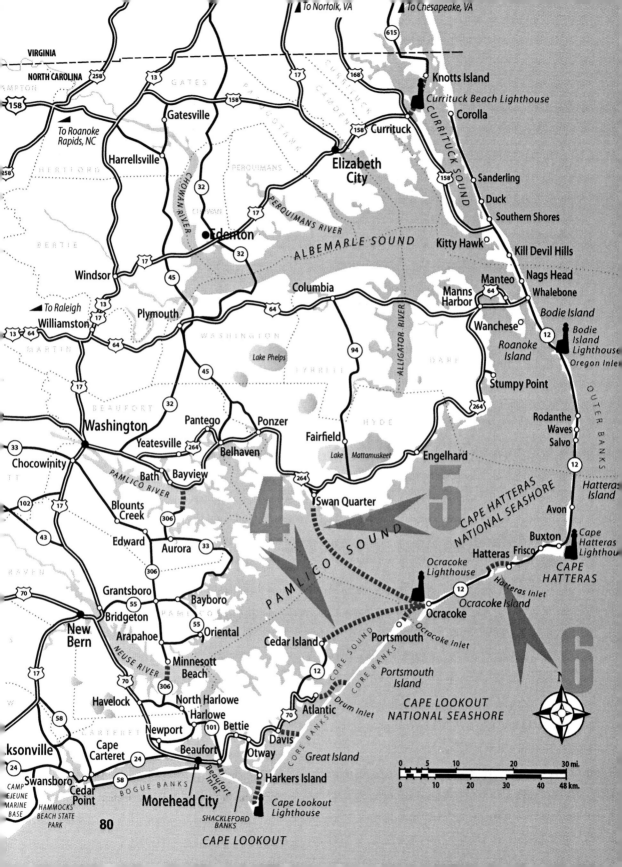

Washington, NC, to Swan Quarter ferry landing
From downtown Washington, take US 264 E for 29 miles east through communities of Bunyan, Yeatesville, and Pantego to the town of Belhaven. Outside Belhaven, turn left (east) on US 264 and proceed for 9.2 miles, crossing the Pungo River to the intersection with NC 45 at the flashing traffic signal in the Ponzer community. Keep to the right and continue on US 264 / NC 45 for another 15.1 miles, through the community of Rose Bay, to the turnoff for Swan Quarter. Follow the ferry signs, bearing right onto NC 45 S / T. G. "Sonny Boy" Joyner Hwy. Proceed 2.1 miles and turn left onto NC 45 / Main St. Make an immediate right turn on SR 1128/45 (Oyster Creek Rd.) and proceed 0.4 miles, turning right at the ferry road.
Total est. distance: 56 miles
Total est. time: 1 hour, 20 minutes

Manns Harbor, NC (Dare County mainland) to Swan Quarter ferry landing
Take US 84/US 264/US 64 for 1.6 miles until the turnoff for U S264. Turn left and continue on US 264 south for 60 miles, past the Alligator River National Wildlife Refuge and the communities of Stumpy Point and Engelhard, past Lake Mattamuskeet. Turn left onto US 264 / NC 94 / Main St. on the outskirts of Swan Quarter and continue to follow Main St. 1.5 miles to the center of town. Turn left onto SR 1128/45 (Oyster Creek Rd.) and proceed 0.4 miles, turning right at the ferry road.
Total est. distance: 63.5 miles
Total est. time: 1 hour 30 minutes

Ocracoke ferry landing (N) to Ocracoke ferry landing (S)
From the ferry travel NC 12 southwest for 19.3 miles. At the village of Ocracoke, turn right and proceed 0.7 miles around Silver Lake to the ferry landing.
Total est. distance: 20 miles
Total est. time: 35–40 minutes, depending on traffic

Off Season

Departs Ocracoke	Departs Hatteras
JAN 1, 2007 – APRIL 28, 2007	
Departs Hatteras and Ocracoke every hour, 5 am – midnight	

Ocracoke–Hatteras SCHEDULE

ALL DATES AND TIMES
SUBJECT TO CHANGE
CALL 1.800.BY-FERRY

Map and directions, pp. 92–93

Shoulder Season

OCT 30, 2007 – DEC 31, 2007

Departs Ocracoke	Departs Hatteras
5.00 am	5.00 am
6.00 am	6.00 am
7.00 am	7.00 am
8.00 am	8.00 am
9.00 am	9.00 am
10.00 am	10.00 am
10.30 am	10.30 am
11.00 am	11.00 am
11.30 am	11.30 am
12.00 noon	12.00 noon
12.30 pm	12.30 pm
1.00 pm	1.00 pm
1.30 pm	1.30 pm
2.00 pm	2.00 pm
2.30 pm	2.30 pm
3.00 pm	3.00 pm
3.30 pm	3.30 pm
4.00 pm	4.00 pm
4.30 pm	4.30 pm
5.00 pm	5.00 pm
6.00 pm	6.00 pm
7.00 pm	7.00 pm
8.00 pm	8.00 pm
9.00 pm	9.00 pm
10.00 pm	10.00 pm
11.00 pm	11.00 pm
12.00 midnight	12.00 midnight

High Season

MAY 1, 2007 – OCT 29, 2007

Departs Ocracoke	Departs Hatteras
5.00 am	5.00 am
6.00 am	6.00 am
7.00 am	7.00 am
---	7.30 am
8.00 am	8.00 am
8.30 am	8.30 am
9.00 am	9.00 am
9.30 am	9.30 am
10.00 am	10.00 am
10.30 am	10.30 am
11.00 am	11.00 am
11.30 am	11.30 am
12.00 noon	12.00 noon
12.30 pm	12.30 pm
1.00 pm	1.00 pm
1.30 pm	1.30 pm
2.00 pm	2.00 pm
2.30 pm	2.30 pm
3.00 pm	3.00 pm
3.30 pm	3.30 pm
4.00 pm	4.00 pm
4.30 pm	4.30 pm
5.00 pm	5.00 pm
5.30 pm	5.30 pm
6.00 pm	6.00 pm
6.30 pm	6.30 pm
7.00 pm	7.00 pm
8.00 pm	8.00 pm
9.00 pm	9.00 pm
10.00 pm	10.00 pm
11.00 pm	11.00 pm
12.00 midnight	12.00 midnight

6 Ocracoke– Hatteras

vehicle/passenger ferry

route NC Hwy 12; crosses Hatteras Inlet from northern end of **Ocracoke Island** (pop. 750, Hyde County) to village of **Hatteras** (pop. 634, Dare County) on southern end of Hatteras Island

duration 40 min

distance 3.3 mi

vessels/capacity Hatteras Class (30 vehicles, 149 passengers): M/V *Cape Point*, M/V *Chicamacomico*, M/V *Frisco*, M/V *Kinnakeet*, M/V *Ocracoke*, M/V *Thomas A. Baum*; River Class (40 vehicles, 300 passengers): M/V *Croatoan*, M/V *Hatteras*, M/V *W. Stanford White*

fare Free

reservations No

terminal
Ocracoke
1.800.345.1665
252.928.3841
Hatteras 1.800.368.8949
252.986.2353
Web www.ncferry.org

current updates May be monitored on radio channel WPLS 1060 AM in the vicinity of the Hatteras landing

shore facilities Ocracoke: Comfort station with restrooms, vending, water fountains Hatteras Inlet: Visitor center with office, Ship's Store, restrooms, vending machines; proximity to Hatteras Landing retail

fact During the busy summer season the ferry service operates 10 boats simultaneously at peak times.

THE FIRST SATURDAY IN JUNE IS A *popular day for island-hopping from Ocracoke to Hatteras. The M/V* Thomas A. Baum *is already full and on its way as we arrive—but at this otherwise deserted end of the island, the boats load every fifteen minutes or so. There's time to climb the top of the dune overlooking Hatteras Inlet and watch for the next one to arrive.*

At the isolated northern ferry terminal on Ocracoke, a comfort station is a welcome sight to travelers.

"Everybody thinks that Hatteras Inlet is going to be busiest on Saturdays and Sundays, and those are our slowest days," says one Ferry Division staffer. "Tuesdays are a busy day for us. People check into their cabins or their houses on Sunday, they get sunburned on Monday, and Tuesday they're looking to do something else."

On this particular route, which departs from the far northern tip of narrow Ocracoke Island, people arrive at the end of Highway 12 with no other option except the ferry. "People just hop on the boat and they say, 'Where does it go?'" says deckhand S. D. Smith onboard the Kinnakeet.

Smith tells me how the crew get their start. Although no prior experience as ferry operator, or even in the Coast Guard, is required for an entry-level job, applicants pass the test for ordinary seaman. From there, a seaman can work up to able seaman in two years, and to mate in another two. It takes a long time to gain experience, and because people in the ferry service tend to stay there, it can take an especially long time to advance.

Many inside the ferry organization feel the pay isn't competitive, though the work can be rewarding. On the Outer Banks, the cost of living has increased so much that it's outpaced the capacity of locals to live there, so most crew members live on the mainland and commute out to work on the island ferries.

Smith takes me up to the bridge for a special treat: the chance to spend a few minutes with Captain Sue Garrett, the first woman to be certified as a captain in the North Carolina Ferry System. Captain Garrett sports a dark tan and a ready smile. After starting as a deckhand in 1980, she earned her AB a few years later and her captain's license in due time. She's primarily responsible for the run here at Hatteras, though she helped out with the hurricane relief run from Stumpy Point to Hatteras after Isabel. In her spare time she tends to a couple of Banker ponies; her husband, Steve, runs a charter boat, the Gambler, out of Hatteras.

So what was it like to be the first woman captain? I ask. It's not a new question to her. Garrett has been interviewed by scads of newspapers, especially back when she was first appointed. But these days she's not the only female skipper working with the fleet; another has joined the ferry service at Southport–Fort Fisher.

"Guess I'll have to start sharing the limelight now," Garrett says with good humor. I'll look into that, I tell her—we're approaching port at Hatteras, and I have to let the captain get back to guiding the vessel.

But if you want to know more about Sue Garrett and her career with the ferry system, get your hands on Linda E. Nunn's June 2002 story from the Island Breeze, "Aye, Aye, Captain, Ma'am!"

WHEN YOU DRIVE OFF THE ferry at the Hatteras terminal, you're at the southern end of a bow-shaped string of three islands connected by one highway, NC 12, that stretches north for 60 miles before encountering an intersection with another thoroughfare. (Bicyclists: you'll have to share the two lanes of asphalt with cars—there's no marked bike lane.)

Much of the Outer Banks oceanfront is designated as the **Cape Hatteras National Seashore,** and many of those miles are blessedly unpopulated and undeveloped. To enjoy your Outer Banks trip to fullest advantage, stay stocked on food, gas, and cash, as these commodities won't always be there where or when you run out.

That's not to say that the entire length of the Outer Banks is desolate and primitive—upscale communities from Hatteras to Corolla offer some of the most luxurious living money can buy, and the northern stretch of Bodie Island between Nags Head and Kitty Hawk typifies dense resort development and commercial tourist sprawl.

History. The strategically located Outer Banks islands attracted European explorers and settlers from the time of Sir Walter Raleigh in 1585, when England and Spain vied for mastery of the new world. Though

Raleigh's colony at Roanoke Island mysteriously failed (the basis of the outdoor drama *The Lost Colony* and much other local history), the British eventually gained control of the entire region and claimed it for King Charles as Carolina.

Naval exploration, merchant shipping, and eventually fishing and whaling in the nearby Gulf Stream brought large numbers of ships and boats to Outer Banks and inland ports. But treacherous weather and water conditions were always a risk, as were pirates suchs as the infamous Blackbeard, captured and executed at Ocracoke in 1718.

Lighthouses and, later, lifesaving stations were established along the chain of islands to protect vessels and occupants from extensive shoals and shallows and from violent storms. Despite such measures the Outer Banks earned a fearful reputation as "the Graveyard of the Atlantic": more than 2,000 ships, over four centuries, are known to have wrecked here.

Far-flung communities of hardy folk flourished at ports, inlets, fishing villages, and haulovers (narrow stretches of land where cargoes could be transported by wagon from oceangoing ships on the Atlantic to shallower-draft boats on the sound side).

As hurricanes opened new inlets or destroyed settlements, however, some towns never recovered successfully. Some, like Portsmouth on the Core Banks, were abandoned entirely.

Year-round residents who remained, in families such as the Midgettes and Babbs,

The ferry rounding the point of Ocracoke Island at Hatteras Inlet

turned to fishing, boatbuilding, and rescue operations for a living. Their expertise became increasingly valuable once again in the twentieth century as tourists discovered the islands for sportfishing and hunting. Once regular ferry service was established in the 1940s and bridges were constructed from the northern mainland, motor vehicles had ready access to the islands—as long as the road wasn't overwashed by the sea or blocked by storm-shifting dunes.

As barrier islands, the Outer Banks take the brunt of the ocean's fury, their tall, windswept dunes creating a peaceful and protected haven on the sound side. The islands have also shielded the mainland during times of war: in the Civil War, providing cover for Southern blockade runners, and in the two world wars fending off German submarine and U-boat attacks. During World War II a stretch of the Outer Banks became known

Bicycles and kayaks: two excellent ways to experience the Outer Banks. On the northern end, a bike path stretches from Duck to Corolla.

as Torpedo Junction for the constant threat from enemy craft—as well as the number sunk by U.S. defenses.

Technological history was made in 1903 at Kitty Hawk, on the northern Outer Banks, when Orville and Wilbur Wright accomplished the first manned airplane flight. The high dunes and smooth stretches of sand were ideal for their experiments—as they still are today for recreational kite-fliers and hang-gliders.

Today, the Outer Banks thrive on **outdoor recreation,** from canoeing, kayaking, sailing, surfing, parasailing, and every other imaginable permutation of wind-and-water sports, to birdwatching, beachcombing, camping, and hiking. The islands' proximity to the Gulf Stream makes the Outer Banks a major destination for offshore angling—for snapper, dolphin, grouper, triggerfish, and sea bass, as well as sportfishing for mackerel and sailfish. Inshore waters yield flounder, bluefish, spot, striper, red drum, and croaker, among many other sought-after species.

For visitors inclined to **cultural and intellectual activities,** the Outer Banks attract artists, writers, and readers, naturalists and historians, and those simply looking for spiritual renewal. Solitary pursuits as well as organized programs fill long summer days or quiet winter ones.

Congress ensured the long-term preservation of this unique natural area when, in 1953, it designated it as the country's first national seashore.

Hatteras (the village, which is located on Hatteras Island a few miles from the geographical Cape Hatteras) has a grocery store and several gas stations. Although ferry service did not run to this remote fishing village until after World War II and Highway 12 was not extended here until the 1950s, Hatteras has definitely seen an influx of new residents in recent years. Adjacent to the ferry, Hatteras Landing is a new, exclusive marina and residential development. The Old Station on NC 12 is the last chance for gas and provisions before boarding the Ocracoke-bound ferry.

Past the communities of **Frisco** and **Buxton** is the **Hatteras Island Visitor Center,** gateway to the famous spiral-striped lighthouse that was moved further inland in 1999 to save it from the encroaching surf. The lighthouse—the tallest in the nation—is open during designated hours, and those willing and able may climb the 260-plus steps to the top for an awe-inspiring vista of dunes and ocean. Other exhibits, buildings, trails, beaches, and interpretive programs make for a full and engaging day.

Throughout the islands are clustered motels, condominiums, and rental houses. Private campgrounds and RV parks offer amenities from the rustic to the high-tech. The National Park Service operates popular but more basic campgrounds at Ocracoke; at Frisco and Cape Point on Hatteras Island; and at Oregon Inlet on Bodie Island.

Northward along the ribbon of Highway 12, each small community has its own distinct history and personality. In **Avon, Salvo, Waves,** and **Rodanthe** (Ro-DAN-thuh), you'll find a scattering of historic sites,

The Cape Hatteras Lighthouse, moved 1,600 feet from the ocean in 1999, is one of North Carolina's most enduring symbols.

fishing piers, small supermarkets, hardware stores, recreational otufitters, boutiques, and general shopping—and sometimes an open gas station. In between you'll find majestic expanses of sand dunes and sea oats. The **Pea Island Wildlife Refuge** occupies the northern stretch of Hatteras Island; there is an excellent nature trail on the sound side (don't forget the bug spray).

At **Oregon Inlet,** the Herbert C. Bonner Bridge now connects Hatteras and Bodie Islands, where one of the state's first ferry operations formerly ran. With its marina and a major Coast Guard facility, Oregon Inlet constitutes the heart of Outer Banks boating and fishing; scores of charter boats are based here.

Bodie Island's (pronounce it either "body" or BOE-dy) lighthouse is the one marked by horizontal black and white bands. A Park Service visitor center and nature trail are located adjacent to the lighthouse; nearby is Coquina Beach, one of the seashore's handful of swimming beaches with bathhouse facilities and lifeguards in summer.

At **Whalebone Junction**, US Highway 264 links by bridge to Roanoke Island, Manns Harbor on the Dare County mainland, and points west. (There are only two highway routes to the Outer Banks: NC 168 and US 158 from Norfolk, Va., and Elizabeth City via the Wright Memorial Bridge to Kitty Hawk; and US 64/264 from Raleigh via mainland Dare County and the Washington Baum Bridge.)

Whalebone marks the divide between the sparsely and densely populated portions of the Outer Banks. Gas and food are readily available at the junction.

On **Roanoke Island**, the names of the two principal towns, **Manteo** and **Wanchese,** honor the two Indians who accompanied Sir Walter Raleigh to England in the 1500s and returned to tribal honors and, ultimately, differing views on the wisdom of coopera-

tion between Native Americans and white settlers. The town of Manteo, home of Fort Raleigh and, since 1953, *The Lost Colony* outdoor drama, is best known for its tourist hospitality and culture; Wanchese (WAHN-cheese), for fishing and boating.

Food and lodging on the island range from touristy to elegant and are readily available; downtown Manteo is home to several distinctive waterfront inns.

If you were to continue north on NC 12 at Whalebone, you'd encounter **Nags Head, Kill Devil Hills,** and **Kitty Hawk** in one indistinguishable strip of four-lane. Name any national hotel or motel chain, any fast-food or casual-dining franchise, any big-box retailer or outlet store: chances are it's represented here.

For a more idiosyncratic experience, consider lodgings at the International Youth Hostel, off the beaten path at Kitty Hawk. (Better be sure you're on friendly terms with peacocks.) Visit Kitty Hawk Kites. Climb the dunes (highest on the East Coast) and investigate the marsh at Jockey's Ridge State Park. Take in the scenery from the white-granite Wright Brothers Memorial.

If you're of a mind to see the northern-most of the Outer Banks lighthouses, continue north on NC 12 at the curve in Kitty Hawk where most traffic follows the Wright Memorial Bridge to the mainland. In the communities of **Southern Shores, Duck,** and **Corolla,** commercial development isn't as jam-packed as it is on the four-lane, but high-end residential real estate and upscale amenties have changed the face of this beachfront area drastically in the past two decades.

At Corolla (kuh-RAH-lah), the red-brick Currituck Beach Lighthouse, completed in 1875, is open to visitors. The Whalehead Club, once a private hunting lodge, is the focal point of the Currituck Heritage Park, which is run by the nonprofit Whalehead Preservation Trust and open to the public for tours, events, and recreation.

The restored Whalehead Club, now open to the public for tours and events as part of the Currituck Heritage Park, was once one of the most elegant hunting clubs on the northern Outer Banks.

Although the narrow spit of land known as the **Currituck Outer Banks** is continuous from North Carolina into Virginia, there is no public road access between the two states. For non–permit-holders, the road ends at Corolla. (For more on the real estate and access history of this part of the country, see the *Insider's Guide to the Outer Banks.*)

For a while, a new passenger ferry route was under consideration to connect Corolla with the county seat of Currituck, initially for the primary purpose of transporting Outer Banks children to school on the mainland. But the opening of a new school in Corolla has largely addressed that need, and a series of setbacks put an end to the plan. Some Currituck citizens are convinced a lengthy bridge is the inevitable long-term solution.

Reading. North Carolina's Outer Banks have inspired many books—fiction, mystery, history, poetry, children's books—too many to list. But an enjoyable starting point might be *An Outer Banks Reader* (1998), edited by David Stick, who published the classic history *The Outer Banks of North Carolina* in 1958. Judge Charles Harry Whedbee compiled several collections of Outer Banks ghost stories and legends from the 1960s until his death in 1990; his books remain in print from John F. Blair Publishers. Molly Perkins Harrison gathered an engaging batch of anecdotes spanning the centuries in *It Happened on the Outer Banks* (2005). Other personal favorites are Anne Russell's children's book *Seabiscuit: Wild Pony of the Outer Banks* (2001); Bland Simpson's *Ghost Ship of Diamond Shoals: The Mystery of the Carroll A. Deering* (2002); Jan DeBlieu's

The Currituck Beach Lighthouse and the lighthouse keeper's cottage are preserved by a community group on a serene site at Corolla.

The Visitors Bureau operates three visitor centers: Whalebone Junction, Manteo, and Kitty Hawk.

For a thorough overview of Outer Banks culture and a wealth of tourist information, spend a few moments at the Aycock Brown Welcome Center, at the curve on US 158 in Kitty Hawk—and a few minutes longer on the center's inviting nature trail; call 252.261.4644.

Hatteras Journal (1998), a story of her year-long nature study of the island; and David Wright and David Zoby's *Fire on the Beach* (2001), a history of an all-black unit of the U.S. Life-Saving Service on Pea Island.

For more information
• Outer Banks Visitors Bureau, www.outerbanks.org, 252.473.2138 or 1.877.OBX-4FUN (629.4386); information@outerbanks.org

Blue crabs are abundant in the tidal waters of North Carolina's sounds.

Above: End of the road, on the Currituck Outer Banks north of Corolla. Below: Pilings at the ferry dock

Ocracoke–Hatteras GETTING THERE

**Ocracoke ferry landing (S) to Ocracoke
ferry landing (N) and Hatteras ferry**
From the ferry landing at Ocracoke, follow Silver
Lake Rd. 0.7 miles around Silver Lake to the village
of Ocracoke. Turn left onto NC 12 / Irvin S. Garrish
Hwy. Follow NC 12 northeast for 19.3 miles, past
the Ocracoke campground and the pony pasture to
the far northern end of the island. Loop around to
the left to enter the line for the Hatteras ferry.
Total est. distance: 20 miles
Total est. time: 35–40 minutes, depending on
traffic

Nags Head, NC, to Hatteras Inlet ferry landing
From the center of Nags Head, take US 158 E / S.
Croatan Hwy. south for 3.7 miles. At Whalehead
Junction at the intersection with US 264, which
will turn right toward Roanoke Island, turn left
onto NC 12 S. Proceed 57.7 miles south on Bodie
Island, across the Herbert C. Bonner bridge over
Oregon Inlet, to Pea Island and Hatteras Island.
At the town of Buxton, NC 12 will bear left; stay
on NC 12 through Frisco to Hatteras Village. Bear
right and continue 0.7 miles to the ferry landing.
Total est. distance: 62 miles
Total est. time: 1 hour 30 minutes to 2 hours,
under ideal traffic and weather conditions

Note that from **Kill Devil Hills to Hatteras Inlet,**
the distance is 75 miles. Mile markers along NC
12, starting from the north, are commonly used for
directions and reference on the Outer Banks.

The Herbert C. Bonner Bridge over Oregon Inlet,
bulkheads of old ferry landing in foreground

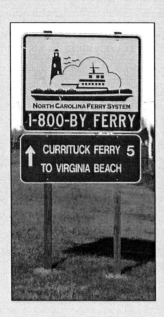

Currituck–Knotts Island SCHEDULE

ALL DATES AND TIMES
SUBJECT TO CHANGE
CALL 1.800.BY-FERRY

**Map and directions,
pp. 100–101**

Departs Currituck	Departs Knotts Island
Year-round schedule	
6.00 am	---
---	7.00 am
9.00 am	
---	10.00 am
11.00 am	---
---	12.00 noon
1.00 pm	---
---	2.00 pm
3.30 pm	---
---	4.30 pm
*5.30 pm	---
---	6.30 pm
*Departs at 5.45 when school is in session	

The Old Currituck Jail, a historic landmark within a few yards of the ferry landing

CHAPTER 7

Currituck–Knotts Island

vehicle/passenger ferry

route Crosses North Landing River/Intracoastal Waterway from town of **Currituck** (pop. 700, Currituck County) to town of **Knotts Island** (pop. 1,825, Currituck County)

duration 45 min

distance 4.3 mi

vessels Old River Class (20 vehicles, 149 passengers): M/V Gov. James Baxter Hunt

fare Free

reservations No

terminal Currituck 252.232.2683 Web www.ncferry.org

shore facilities Currituck: Ferry office, restrooms, water fountain, vending, newspaper racks, picnic shelters Knotts Island: restroom

fact The ferry tranposrts students to school on the mainland in half the time of the 90-minute bus route via southern Virginia.

THE TOWN OF CURRITUCK IS A WORLD AWAY *from the determined-recreation bustle of Nags Head on a June weekend. To get there from the Outer Banks requires a drive past Kill Devil Hills and Kitty Hawk, across the Wright Memorial Bridge, where the visitor center marks the entrance to (and our exit from) Vacationland. We travel US 158 up the peninsula, noting the picturesque names: Harbinger. Spot. Bertha. Waterlily. Coinjock.*

We turn off onto the ferry entrance—not an access road, as we've come to expect, but a landing that's more like a town dock, marked only by a wooden gazebo and the colors of the nation, the state, and the ferry system flying on the halyard. We wait for the first ferry of the morning.

Knotts Island is known for its veg-etable, fruit, and berry cultivation, peaches in summer and grape

vineyards in autumn, and it's also the home of Mackay Island Wildlife Refuge, a haven of marsh and forest. It's there that we're headed.

We're first on the boat. Beside us in a white convertible is a sunglassed young woman in a Duke University T-shirt, traveling alone, who's clearly done this crossing before—she has her coffee at the ready, binoculars and paperback on the seat beside her, cell phone in hand. It's a brilliant morning. The sun sparkles off the sound, birds flock and circle, pennants beat with the breeze, the white decks of the ferry gleam. We lean over the rail and look expectantly toward the next appearance of land. In her car, the girl reads. All is peace and quiet.

We're making all speed in open water when I hear the ringtone of a cell phone. It's the girl's. She answers, animatedly grabs the binoculars, opens the car door, and runs to the rail on our side. Off in the distance, to starboard, a sailboat is moving toward the island, and the girl with the phone raises the binoculars in its direction. "Can you see me?" she calls out, yelling as though she could hail the boat from here. "I'm waving!" She lets the binoculars hang around her neck so that one hand is free while she holds the phone with the other.

Their conversation continues only briefly. "I'll see you at the house," she says in closing. She snaps the phone shut. She looks our way, in a mixture of apology and excitement. "My boy-friend," she explains. "We're going sailing with his parents."

I smile at her. "Sounds serious."

She beams back. Whatever you have to look forward to on the other side, it's one gorgeous day on the ferry.

NORTH CAROLINA DIVIDES WITH Southern Virginia a verdant bit of territory nearly surrounded by bays, the North Landing River, and Currituck Sound, called Knotts Island. Along with the Currituck Outer Banks to the east and a slice of mainland to the west, it constitutes Currituck County, North Carolina's northeasternmost corner. The county in some ways gravitates more to Virginia than Carolina—it's included in

Virginia's Hampton Roads metropolitan statistical area, and the *Virginian-Pilot* is the predominant newspaper. To reach it by land requires driving a twisting path across the state line and back. It's a sparsely populated region, too: some 20,000 permanent residents countywide, living in 35 towns and villages spread over 291 square miles (also encompassing nearly as much area in water). But into that compact space it packs a great

Midsummer in the Mackay Island National Wildlife Refuge

deal of natural beauty, wildlife, waterway access, and flourishing agriculture, and this out-of-the-way dot on the map is worth the ferry ride to get there.

Many people who live here commute to the Virginia Beach and Norfolk areas; others work in the tourism industry; many still fish or farm. Duck hunting is big.

On the mainland at **Currituck,** the center of town (not more than a village, though it's the county seat) is within easy walking distance of the ferry landing. The historic Old Currituck Jail, and the current-day courthouse next door, are only a few paces from the off-ramp. The school board office is right down the road; the gas station and grocery store are two-tenths of a mile away.

Note well: If it's the Currituck Outer Banks or the Currituck Beach Lighthouse you're looking for, don't expect to reach it via the ferry that leaves from the town of this name (once you reach Knotts Island, the only road off island takes you into Virginia). To get to the far eastern part of the county, where the beaches are located, you'll need to head down the peninsula across the bridge into Dare County, and drive back up again.

Lodgings in mainland Currituck County and nearby areas are few: B&Bs and small motels in **Grandy, Barco,** and **Moyock,** each about 10 miles from the ferry in different directions. A wider selection will require a drive to **Elizabeth City,** half an hour southwest, or to **Chesapeake, Va.,** or the **Virginia Beach** metropolitan area an hour to the north.

There are a handful of private campgrounds: at Bells Island along the Intracoastal Waterway, and at Grandy and Coin-

All aboard for Knotts Island

jock. Just past the Virginia state line from Knotts Island on Highway 615 (S. Princess Anne Road) is North Landing Beach Campground, a well-run camping and RV park.

Currituck offers a choice of fast food, homestyle dining, or seafood, and all along US 158 and NC 168 there are plenty of eateries featuring regional specialties—such as Eastern North Carolina barbecue dressed with coleslaw (don't miss it!).

Before Prohibition, North Carolina produced more wine than any other state in

Antique shop, US 158

the country. Today, **Knotts Island** is contributing to the state's revitalized reputation as a winegrowing region. Two vineyards, Martin and Moonrise Bay, are accessible by the ferry. Both offer tours and tastings in season.

Knotts Island is still a quiet, slow-paced place. It has only one motel and only one restaurant. About a hundred junior high and high school students travel to school in Currituck via ferry, the big yellow bus bringing students for the 7:00 am run and returning

for them on the 3:30 or the 5:30.

Mackay Island National Wildlife Refuge, established in 1960, encompasses 8,138 acres in both states. It's a great place for birding. Peregrine falcons, a nesting pair of American bald eagles, and concentrations of wading birds, shorebirds, ducks, and geese are found here. ("Currituck" derives, in fact, from a Native American word for goose.) Two nature trails, part of the system named in memory of native North Carolinian Charles Kuralt, meander beside fresh- and saltwater marshes.

Whichever direction you drive from the ferry landings, intriguing vistas of land and water surprise at every turn. North and west, the **Great Dismal Swamp,** with its canals, ditches, and 3,100-acre natural lake, is a wilderness environment unique in the state. The Dismal Swamp Canal Welcome Center in Camden County welcomes visitors by water or land.

North and east, toward Virginia Beach and the Hampton Roads area, Princess Anne Road winds through picture-postcard farmland and hamlets, its antique shops and country stores interspersed with exurban developments.

South on the peninsula, quirky eateries, antique stores, and beckoning lanes dot the five-lane Albemarle Highway (US 158 / Caratoke Highway). In between, billboards tout amenities ranging from the tempting (Outer Banks waterfront lodgings) to the tasteless (I Got My Crabs from Dirty Dick's; Try Our Nuts—you get the idea).

To get in the spirit for traveling in the state's northeasternmost corner, read Bland Simpson and Ann Cary Simpson's *The In-*

ner Islands: A Carolinian's Coastal Plain Chronicle (2007) or his *The Great Dismal: A Carolinian's Swamp Memoir* (1998).

Make time, as well, to immerse yourself in the vivid imagery of *Searching for Virginia Dare: A Fool's Errand* (2002) by Marjorie Hudson, a lyrical investigation into history, culture, and self that's centered around North Carolina's most vexing mystery.

For more information
• Currituck Chamber of Commerce, www.currituckchamber.org, 252.453.9497
• Mackay Island National Wildlife Refuge Highay 615, www.fws.gov/mackayisland, 252.429.3100

Right: Raising the flag by morning light
Below: Ferry docked at the Currituck landing

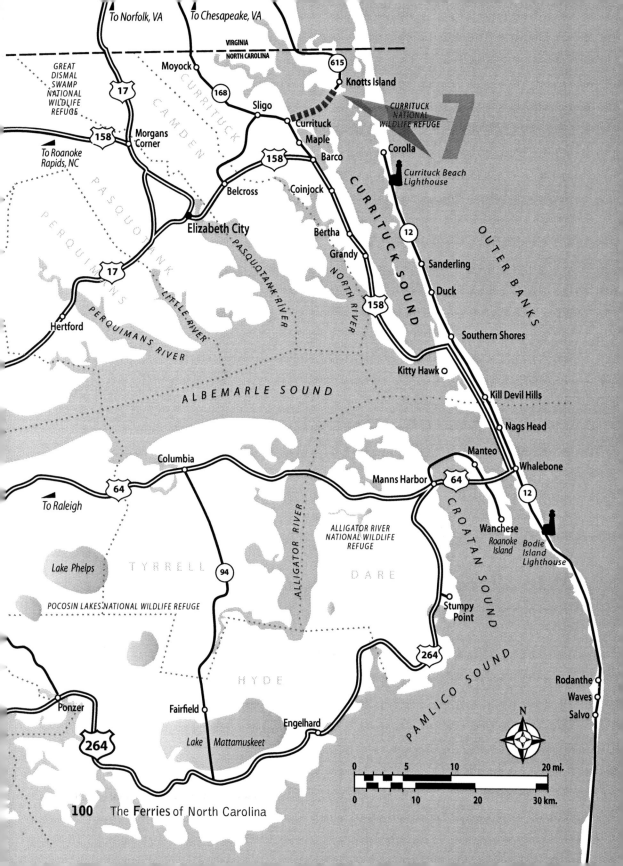

To Norfolk, VA
To Chesapeake, VA

VIRGINIA
NORTH CAROLINA

Moyock

GREAT DISMAL SWAMP NATIONAL WILDLIFE REFUGE

17

168

Sligo

615

Knotts Island

CURRITUCK NATIONAL WILDLIFE REFUGE

Currituck

Maple

Barco

Corolla

Currituck Beach Lighthouse

158

Morgans Corner

To Roanoke Rapids, NC

158

Belcross

Coinjock

CAMDEN

CURRITUCK

PASQUOTANK

PERQUIMANS

Elizabeth City

Bertha

Grandy

158

12

CURRITUCK SOUND

OUTER BANKS

Sanderling

Duck

17

PASQUOTANK RIVER

LITTLE RIVER

NORTH RIVER

Southern Shores

Hertford

PERQUIMANS RIVER

Kitty Hawk

ALBEMARLE SOUND

Kill Devil Hills

Nags Head

Manteo

Whalebone

Columbia

64

Manns Harbor

64

12

To Raleigh

64

ALLIGATOR RIVER

ALLIGATOR RIVER NATIONAL WILDLIFE REFUGE

DARE

CROATAN SOUND

Wanchese

Roanoke Island

Bodie Island Lighthouse

Lake Phelps

TYRRELL

94

POCOSIN LAKES NATIONAL WILDLIFE REFUGE

Stumpy Point

264

PAMLICO SOUND

HYDE

Rodanthe

Waves

Salvo

Ponzer

Fairfield

Engelhard

264

Lake Mattamuskeet

N

0   5   10   20 mi.
0   10   20   30 km.

100 The Ferries of North Carolina

Elizabeth City, NC, to Currituck ferry landing
From downtown Elizabeth City take US 158 E / NC 34 / E. Elizabeth St. northeast across the Pasquotank River bridge. Continue to follow US 158 E for 5.6 miles to the community of Belcross. Stay straight to go onto NC 34 E. Continue 9.2 miles through the communities of Gregory and Shawboro. At the community of Sligo, turn right onto NC 168. Proceed 3.2 miles; turn left onto Courthouse Rd. / NC 1242 and follow signs to ferry landing. (Note that although there is a general sign for the ferry, the turnoff at Courthouse Rd. is not well indicated.)
Total est. distance: 18 miles
Total est. time: 25 minutes

Kitty Hawk, NC, to Currituck ferry landing
From the center of Kitty Hawk on US 158 W / NC 12 N, bear left and cross Wright Memorial Bridge to Point Harbor; proceed 30 miles, continuing north through Jarvisburg and Coinjock. At the village of Barco, stay straight to go onto NC 168. Proceed 4.8 miles to Currituck. Turn left onto Courthouse Rd. / NC 1242 and follow signs to ferry landing. (Note that although there is a general sign for the ferry, the turnoff at Courthouse Rd. is not well indicated.)
Total est. distance: 38 miles
Total est. time: 1 hour

Virginia Beach, VA, to Currituck ferry landing
From downtown Virginia Beach, turn right onto I-264 W / 22nd St. Follow I-264 W 12.6 miles. Merge onto I-64 E / Hampton Roads Belt via the exit on the left toward Chesapeake / Suffolk. Proceed 7.9 miles. At exit 291B, merge onto Martin Luther King Jr. Memorial Hwy. / I-464 S toward VA 104 S / Elizabeth City / US 17 S / Dominion Blvd. / VA 168 S for 0.6 miles. Merge onto VA 168 S via the exit on the left toward Nags Head / Manteo (portions toll). Continue for 29 miles through Saint Brides, Va., across the state line and through Moyock, N.C., to Currituck. Turn left onto Courthouse Rd. / NC 1242 and follow signs to ferry landing. (Note that although there is a general sign for the ferry, the turnoff at Courthouse Rd. is not well indicated.)
Total est. distance: 50 miles
Total est. time: 1 hour, 10 minutes

Virginia Beach, Va., to Knotts Island ferry landing
From its intersection with Gen. Booth Blvd. in Virginia Beach, take VA 615/Princess Anne Rd. south for 21.6 miles, crossing into North Carolina, where the highway becomes NC 615. Make a slight right turn onto NC 615/Knotts Island Rd.; proceed 1.4 miles and turn right on S. End Rd / NC 615. Continue to follow NC 615 to end, 2.1 miles; turn right on Ferry Dock Rd. Ferry landing is 0.4 miles at end of road.
Total est. distance: 33 miles
Total est. time: 1 hour

On Knotts Island, vineyards flank the gate to the Currituck Gunning and Fishing Club.

other **ferries** serving North Carolina's **islands**

RUN YOUR FINGER DOWN THE MAP of North Carolina's 320-mile coastline and count the number of islands that aren't connected by bridge access, and you'll start to appreciate the wealth of environmental, historical, and recreational opportunities afforded by these isolated locales. In years past, communities of settlers and sailors thrived on some of the state's remotest islands despite the elements and the scarcity of daily needs. Today, we're fortunate that many islands are protected as part of our natural heritage. Whether your intent is to study ponies or marine life, search for seashells, fish at dawn, climb a lighthouse, or camp in the wilderness, the first question is how to get there.

Privately contracted vessels operating on demand or on scheduled runs make it possible for visitors to reach islands not accessible by car. (Be forewarned that cars won't generally be found on the other side, either.)

Private toll ferries will take you to the luxurious (think Bald Head Island) or the primitive (like Hammocks Beach). To the populous (the city of Wilmington, where a ten-minute river taxi carries folks to Eagles Island and the Battleship *North Carolina*) or to the deserted (the ghost town of Portsmouth, served by ferry from nearby Ocracoke). To the diminutive (47-acre Sugarloaf, across from Morehead City waterfront) or to the daunting (the 56 miles of the Cape Lookout National Seashore).

Ferries operated via concessions with the National Park Service provide visitors a way to reach uninhabited islands such as Shackleford Banks.

Conveyances are as varied as small open skiffs, three-deck catamarans, canopied pon-

Once you're on the islands, transportation options and facilities vary.

toon boats, and oversized speedboats.

Schedules and rates are complicated, according to seasons, weather, and even business conditions and changes in management. And given the array of departure points and destinations, it can be difficult to determine which service best meets your needs.

Planning your trip

It won't be practical to list full details here for every vendor, and boats whose primary purpose is other than transportation, like fishing vessels, pleasure boats and charters, and sightseeing and dinner cruise boats, are beyond the scope of this book. But a bit of general information should set you on the way to a successful trip.

In any case, you should *always* make arrangements for the private ferries in advance by phone. As Captain Rudy Austin, who's made a lifetime of ferrying passengers

around the islands, explains, your captain can advise you about weather conditions, what to bring, and even what's biting on a given day—whether mosquitoes or mullet.

Factors to consider:

• What is the purpose of your trip?

• How long do you want to stay? (For most first-time day visitors to North Carolina's uninhabited islands, four hours is plenty; an overnight stay of any length, whether you're a veteran or a rookie, takes a good deal of special planning.)

• How many are in your party, and what is their level of mobility?

• What necessities will you have to carry over and back—for fun, comfort, and safety?

The chapters in this section are arranged by destination island. Some destinations are accessible from multiple points on the mainland, so you can also rely to an extent on geographical common sense in finding a ride across the water—but don't make the regrettable mistake of arriving at the end of the road on Harkers Island expecting to claim your reservation for Ocracoke!

What to take, and what not to

A day trip on one of the island ferries requires much the same sort of preparation as an extended walk on any trail—you'll want to make sure that your creature comforts are adequately looked after, that you're not burdened down by unnecessary weight, and that you don't get lost or left behind.

Unlike hiking inland or in the mountains, however, you won't be able to count on any source for replenishing fresh water. Nor can you count on ready access to improved toilet facilities (even on developed Bald Head Island, it's easy to find yourself far from public restrooms).

If you're going to be out long enough for the weather to change unexpetedly, ask your ferry operator about emergency procedures.

Do take:

- Water and easy-to-carry food
- Heavy-duty insect repellent. Absolutely necessary!
- Sunscreen and other protection from the elements. A light windbreaker is good even in summer if rain threatens.
- Cap and sunglasses — tightly secured
- Appropriate footwear
- A watch
- A small pack of wet wipes
- A cell phone in case of emergency
- A bag for trash. Don't leave your garbage behind for others.
- Cash for the ferry toll, and a tip if you wish; many operators do not accept checks or credit cards.

Take for fun:

- A camera (covered for protection from spray)
- A notebook and pen. Leave beach reading for other trips — on this one, you won't want the extra weight.
- A bag for gathering shells
- Water toys and beach gear that you can carry easily

Don't take:

- Anything you can't easily carry over soft sand. Even one of those handy-dandy beach carts with big wheels — like we use when camping elsewhere — is more than we wanted to bother with at Portsmouth or Shackleford. And we didn't even want to think about lugging a cooler, however small. When traveling on foot we use an insulated backback with a frozen coolant pack and save all our space for water, which we need lots of.

Take or ask for:

- A map. The ferries usually provide one-page maps to the part of the islands you're visiting. Whether you're on neighborly Bald Head Island or off the beaten path on Portsmouth, you'll be glad for a map that shows landmarks, points of interest, and scale of

Toll ferry service to Cape Lookout National Seashore is provided by licensed private operators on Harkers Island.

miles. Don't walk farther out than you can easily walk back to meet your ferry at the pickup point, and don't underestimate the rate at which young kids tire and slow down after a day at the beach.

Go prepared — and these excursions can be some of the most memorable of your life.

Bald Head Island SCHEDULE

Map and directions, pp. 116–17

The *Ranger,* Bald Head's newest ferry, was added to the fleet in 2006.

Departs Indigo Landing	Departs Bald Head Island
DECEMBER 1–FEBRUARY 28	
*6.00 am	---
---	*6.30 am
*7.00 am	---
	*7.30 am
8.00 am	---
	8.30 am
No ferry at noon except Sun	
	No ferry at 11.30 am except Sun

For most of the year, ferries leave the mainland all day on the hour and the island on the half-hour, from 8 am to 11 pm, skipping one run at midday. Schedules vary slightly according to day of the week, and in winter may be abbreviated as needed.
*Departures before 8 am (and after 9.30 pm) primarily serve Island employees and residents; tram service is not available at those times.

Departs Indigo Landing	Departs Bald Head Island
8.00 pm	
	8:30 pm ThFSat
*10.00 pm	
	*10.30 pm
11.00 pm	---
11.00 pm	

Dowload updated schedule from **www.baldheadisland.com/downloads/ferry_winter.pdf**

Departs Indigo Landing	Departs Bald Head Island
MARCH 1–NOVEMBER 30	
*6.00 am	---
---	*6.30 am
*7.00 am	---
	*7.30 am
8.00 am	---
	8.30 am
No ferry at noon except Sun	
	No ferry at 11.30 am except Sun

For most of the year, ferries leave the mainland all day on the hour and the island on the half-hour, from 8 am to 11 pm, skipping one run at midday. Schedules vary slightly according to day of the week, and in summer may be expanded as needed.
*Departures before 8 am (and after 9.30 pm) primarily serve Island employees and residents; tram service is not available at those times.

Departs Indigo Landing	Departs Bald Head Island
8.00 pm	
---	9.30 pm
*10.00 pm	---
	*10.30 pm
*11.00 pm ThFSat	
	*11.30 pm ThFSat
*Midnight F	

Dowload updated schedule from **www.baldheadisland.com/downloads/ferry_summer.pdf**

Bald Head Island

passenger-only ferry

route Crosses mouth of Cape Fear River from town of **Southport** (pop. 2,605, Brunswick County) to **Bald Head Island** (pop. 225, Brunswick County)

duration 20 min

distance 3 mi

vessels *Adventure, Patriot, Ranger, Revenge, Sans Souci* (maximum capacity 149 passengers, 24 cargo dollies)

fare Adult, round trip, $15
Child ages 3–12, $8
No charge for children under 3
Additional fees for bicycles or other cargo may apply

reservations Suggested (confirm three days in advance) 1.800.234.1666
910.457.5003

terminal
Indigo Plantation
6099 Indigo Plantation Dr.
Southport NC 28461

Bald Head Island Marina
dockmaster 910.457.7380

Web www.baldheadisland.com

shore facilities Indigo: Parking, reception center, restrooms, vending, newspapers, coffee
Bald Head Island Marina: restaurants, lodging, marina store, restrooms, showers, visitor information, cart and bicycle rentals, boutique retail

ferrycam
www.baldheadisland.com/island/web_cam.asp

THE PASSENGERS ON THE 7:00 A.M. *weekday ferry are a mix of BHI residents, service workers employed on the island, day-trippers, and vacationers. People carry on pets, sports equipment, fishing poles, laptop computers, groceries, a kite, and even musical instruments. This has our curiosity piqued.*

Workers bring their equipment: tool belts, power tools, a sack of paint pigment. Each workman has his six-pack–sized cooler for lunch. Veteran travelers on this route stow their larger items on the baggage carts, the weight visibly dropping from their shoulders and their faces as they board the gleaming white boat.

The Patriot *pushes away from the Indigo dock and heads slowly into the Intracoastal Waterway. Once we pass the river pilots' anchorage at Southport, we pick up speed crossing the choppy mouth of the Cape Fear River. For centuries this body of water, with its shifting shoals, has proved difficult for ships to navigate, but the sleek catamaran ferry makes it look easy. It's a short ride till we pass between the bulkheads at the entry to the Bald Head harbor and marina. The* Sans Souci, *one of the other BHI ferries, is docked there, awaiting its opposite run.*

The ferry is the only access, aside from helicopter or private boat, to this resort and residential community three miles from the mainland. The island's elegant showplace homes, uncrowded beaches, sculpted golf course and croquet greensward, and winding cart paths make it a town like nowhere else in the Carolinas. Bald Head Island's developers wanted to create an enclave where visitors would truly feel separated from the daily concerns of the larger world.

Some folks feel it's not possible to build so extensively on a barrier island without forever marring the environment, but to the extent that it can be done, the Mitchell brothers of Bald Head Island Limited have done it very well.

Arriving at the marina dock, passengers scatter to their various destinations: workers to construction sites; residents to family and friends waiting to whisk them away in golf carts; guests, like us, to our island adventure.

Twelve hours later, following a full day of getting to know the island by bicycle, we check in at the ferry dock for the ride home, camera full of photos and notebook full of impressions. On the evening return trip, the painters and drywall finishers and restaurant workers lean against the ferry rail, relaxing and joking. The captain and mate haul in the lines. The members of the string quartet—now dressed in formalwear, even in the summer's heat—loosen their ties and enjoy the breeze on the open water. An afternoon wedding on the island, they explain.

For all of us, a long day's work. But if you have to be on the job on a beautiful June day, hey, what an office.

"Old Baldy," the Bald Head Island lighthouse, is North Carolina's oldest; it was commissioned by Thomas Jefferson and built in 1817.

A VISIT TO **BALD HEAD ISLAND** requires a bit of forethought and advance arrangement (even for those who own property here)—but once you arrive, you forget all about schedules, planning, calendars, noise, traffic, and other irritants of the mainland workaday world. Book your day passage or weekend lodgings, call ahead to arrange for your groceries and bike rental, and carry your duffle stuffed with a few casual clothes, swimsuit, sunscreen, camera, and a good book aboard the ferry with you, and you're set for a sojourn in paradise.

estate tour package called Weekend Passport and overnight accomodations at the Marsh Harbour Inn or Theodosia's Bed & Breakfast (named for the daughter of Aaron Burr pre-

Waters of the Cape Fear River empty into the Atlantic Ocean at the southern tip of Bald Head Island

(Oh, and one other thing you'll need to take with you: a healthy wallet. The fourteen miles of beaches are free—but most other amenities involve some cost and aren't designed for the no-frills traveler.)

Although it's certainly possible to enjoy a day trip to Bald Head, the island is primarily designed as a residential and resort home community, so the ideal way to experience it is a vacation-length stay. **Rental cottages** are priced by the week in high season, shoulder season, and off-season, and Bald Head has a wonderfully different ambience throughout the changing year.

The resort agency also offers a real-

sumed to have perished at sea off the North Carolina barrier islands in 1812).

Aside from these choices—or staying aboard your yacht in the marina—there are no hotels, camping, or other accomodations for impulse visitors. When you book your departure passage on the ferry, you'll also reserve a designated return time. All fares for visitors are round-trip.

Bald Head Island instituted its own **ferry service** in 1984 (replacing an earlier ferry that served the island's few residents), the year after Kent and Mark Mitchell began to acquire land for development. Its first ferry vessel was the *Adventure,* a refitted

utility craft. A mainland terminal was built at Moore's Creek in Southport that same year. In 1987 the *Revenge* was put into service, increasing the number of daily departures.

The *Patriot*, a catamaran custom-designed for the island run, was added soon afterwards and the *Sans Souci* in 1991, a year after the construction of mainland terminal facilities at Indigo Plantation. In 2006, another catamaran, the *Ranger*, was introduced.

The *Sans Souci* docks at Indigo Landing to load visitors and cargo for Bald Head Island

The name of each vessel recalls a bit of North Carolina maritime history. In the eighteenth century, when pirates plied the coast and hid their ships and treasures along Carolina's creeks, the *Queen Anne's Revenge* was the flagship of Blackbeard's flotilla. (Stede Bonnet, the "gentleman pirate," also named his ship the *Revenge*.) But in 1718 Blackbeard and another of his ships, the *Adventure,* met his match in an encounter at Ocracoke with a British force under Lt. Robert Maynard and the original *Ranger.*

Nearly a century later the barque *Patriot* was making a coastwise run from Charleston to New York when it disappeared off the Carolina coast, with Theodosia Burr Alston as passenger.

As for the *Sans Souci,* the former dinner cruise boat already carried that name when it was purchased and refitted for ferry service at Bald Head. But the name just happens to coincide with that of an early plantation of the region—not to mention that of the Cashie River ferry in Bertie County (see chapter 16). Its meaning, French for "without care," suits the island in any case.

Bald Head employs three Coast Guard-licensed ferry crews (including five captains), who alternate three days on, three days off, working a morning shift from 6 am to 3 pm or an evening shift from 3 to 11 pm With a crew of three, the boats carry 99 passengers; with a full complement of four, 149. The ferries run 365 days a year, except in extreme weather conditions; running at 20 to 25 knots, they take a little less than twenty minutes from dock to dock.

People often ask Captain Joe Miller if he ever gets bored, making this same short round trip nine or ten times daily. Not a bit, he says—"It's either very beautiful because it's calm, or very exciting because it's rough."

Miller, who ran ferryboats to Bald Head as early as 1978, when there was not even a marina where the 24-foot Pinyans could tie up, has handled everything from medical emergencies to hurricane evacuations. The strangest passengers he ever (almost) transported to the island? "Two llamas for an island resident," Miller says. "But they got skittish when we tried to load them, and we didn't take them aboard."

Captain Chad McHenry was the youngest BHI Ferries crew member to attain his master's license, in 2003, at age nineteen. But he's a seasoned mariner who grew up around his grandfather's boat and began working on the island at fourteen. "You get away from everything" on Bald Head Island, he says. Working his way up to captain on the ferry crossing, he enjoys the ever-changing scenery and challenges on the water—the big Coast Guard ships, the river pilots, the barges.

In 2005 the BHI ferry service carried more than 320,000 passengers and residents to the island. The island community has grown from a marina with an earlier inn and a few private homes when the Mitchells took it over, to a thriving and self-contained municipality of nearly 900 homes and condominiums, some 200 year-round residents, and a full array of public services, from water and sewer to police and fire protection, a post office, medical care, lending library, chapel, and telephone, cable television, and high-speed Internet. The town of Bald Head Island is governed by a village council and mayor; all property owners participate in

Bald Head's ferries run 7 days a week, 365 days a year, and make as many as 46 departures daily in summer.

homeowners' associations managed by Bald Head Island Limited. The island, historically known as Smith Island, comprises more than 12,000 acres, 10,000 of which are designated as nature preserve and protected from any future development.

The passenger ferry takes guests to the Bald Head Island Marina from the Indigo

Ten thousand acres of Bald Head Island set aside as a nature preserve.

Aboard the ferry, you can choose a seat in the downstairs enclosed lounge or the open upper deck. It's a short ride over to the island, with the silhouette of Old Baldy an easy landmark. To the southwest, the taller, striped Oak Island light is also visible.

When you disembark at the **marina**, you'll find yourself in **Harbour Village,** the island's center of commercial activity—a harbor busy with sailing vessels, sportfishing boats, and yachts as well as the resort's own ferries and barges. A guest services center, sales and rental offices, two restaurants, and the dockmaster's office are located within a few steps of the ferry landing. Nearby is the **Island Passage store,** which offers resort clothing and gifts for sale and handles rentals of golf carts, bicycles, canoes, kayaks, and beach gear. On the other side of the marina are located shops for gifts and eats, and the inns.

Landing on the west side of Southport. (For more about the town of Southport and surrounding areas, see chapter 1.) There, long-term parking is available in several lots (a daily fee applies); a bus shuttle service runs continuously during ferry hours. You may want to drive up to the terminal and drop off luggage and pick up tickets before parking, so be sure to allow sufficient extra time.

The ticket booth will confirm your reservation, and you'll place any large luggage, provisions, or sports equipment on cargo trolleys that will be loaded on the ferry. (In case you're wondering, building materials, home furnishings, and other major shipments travel a slightly different route, by barge.) At the landing there is a comfortable lounge with restrooms, telephone, and island visitor information.

Since most lodgings, the resort clubs, the lighthouse and village, and the beaches are not within easy walking distance (especially when you're loaded down with gear), some form of wheels is called for. Electric-powered **golf carts** are the vehicle of choice. If you're staying in a cottage, your rental will likely include the cart that's garaged at your house. The **island tram** will deliver you and your baggage to your accommodations and pick you up at your scheduled time for return. Carts may also be rented at Island Passage.

A map of the island (in your guest packet or available at the visitor center) is essential for finding

The Hammocks cottages feature the vernacular design typical of Bald Head Island's residential architecture.

your way around Bald Head's miles of cart paths, trails, and streams. Beaches, services, and clusters of homes are dispersed among wild stretches of marshland, high dunes, and maritime forest. In the daytime, be mindful of other vehicles and pedestrians, especially during busy arrival and departure hours; after dusk, watch for animals.

If commuting in your mainland car with windows rolled up is your usual routine, you'll be amazed at the sights, sounds, and smells of the island when experienced from the open cart or bike. From the vista of the dunes overlooking Frying Pan Shoals to the quiet intensity of the live-oak maritime forest, Bald Head's **diverse environments** invite exploration.

In this habitat that is the northernmost tropical zone on the East Coast are found alligators, along with deer, fox, coyote, otter, and other small mammals. Birds are plentiful, from peregrine falcons, warblers and painted buntings in summer, and the occasional bald eagle to ospreys, egrets, and

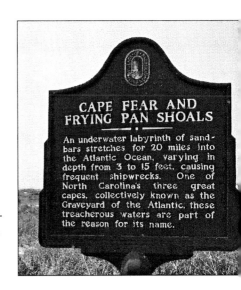

CAPE FEAR AND FRYING PAN SHOALS

An underwater labyrinth of sandbars stretches for 20 miles into the Atlantic Ocean, varying in depth from 3 to 15 feet, causing frequent shipwrecks. One of North Carolina's three great capes, collectively known as the Graveyard of the Atlantic, these treacherous waters are part of the reason for its name.

Nature programs hosted by the Bald Head Island Conservancy introduce participants to the island's environment and abundant wildlife.

Shopping opportunities are limited but interesting, from the boutiques nestled around the marina to the golf pro shop to the mid-island **Maritime Market**, which serves as the island's grocery and general store.

Sports and recreation facilities for owners and vacation renters are first-rate: take your pick of golf, tennis, swimming, croquet, volleyball, bicycling, running, surfing, boating, fishing, and paddling. A day-sailing charter offers excursions and lessons; charter fishing boats venture out as far as the Gulf Stream. The traditionally elegant Bald Head Island Club includes a fine-dining restaurant and a pro shop adjacent to the championship golf course. The posh new Shoals Club, with its starkly dramatic water views, serves lunch and dinner overlooking a swimming pool that blends almost seamlessly with the Atlantic beyond.

White-sand **beaches** surround Bald Head Island on three sides, though with so much shore to offer, none of them are protected by lifeguards. Restroom and changing facilities are few; bathhouses are open to members only. Plans are in the works for improvements to enhance comforts for beachgoers.

other shore and waterbirds. Mosquitoes make their presence well known (prepare for them); butterflies are abundant in summer.

But the star of the nature show on Bald Head Island is the loggerhead turtle. The island's beaches are prime nesting ground for this endangered species, and the nonprofit Bald Head Island Conservancy helps research and protect the turtles.

If your interests run more to species of the homo sapiens variety, Bald Head hosts a schedule of planned social events from Easter egg hunts to Fourth of July fireworks, home tours to wine tastings, croquet matches to musical events, regattas to road races to fishing rodeos. Special activities for children are scheduled throughout the summer. The island is also a popular site for weddings.

Not everything here is sparkling and brand-new, though. Bald Head's **history** dates back well before European exploration and settlement. The Cape Fear Indians inhabited the island, finding abundant hunting and shellfishing. By the time of the American

Veteran captain Rodney Melton, with three decades in service with the BHI ferries, aboard the *Ranger,* the newest of Bald Head's ferry fleet

Revolution, military outfits had come to realize the strategic positioning of Smith Island (as the larger land mass is known); British regiments camped there, as would Confederate troops years later during the Civil War.

In the age of sail, oceangoing and coastwise ships had to navigate Frying Pan Shoals, with its erratic shallows and conflicting currents. A lighthouse was erected on Smith Island in 1817 to warn ships away from the area. A second light, the Cape Fear Lighthouse, was added in 1903, but only its foundations and keepers' quarters survive on Bald Head today, as Captain Charlie's Station. "Old Baldy," as the 1817 light is fondly known, underwent restoration from 1990 to 1993 and today remains the oldest lighthouse in the state. It stands as the focal point of a village not far from the marina that includes the post office, museum, and chapel.

In addition to its strong commitment to preserving history and the natural environment, Bald Head Island also hosts No Boundaries, an innovative art colony that meets on the island every other year. Founded in 1993 as the brainchild of Wilmington visual artists Pamela Toll, Dick Roberts, and Gayle Tustin, No Boundaries invites emerging and renowned artists worldwide to spend a month in residence on the island, working in an atmosphere of international friendship and creative freedom.

Relaxation, exploration, inspiration—the Bald Head Island ferry takes you to all of it. To learn more about Bald Head Island's history and culture, start with David Stick's *Bald Head: A History of Smith Island and Cape Fear* (1985) and his *North Carolina Lighthouses* (1980).

For more information
• Bald Head Island Vacations
1.800.432.RENT
• Bald Head Island Limited
Real Estate 1.800.804.9826
Rentals 1.800.515.1038
www.baldheadisland.com; info@bhisland.com
• Bald Head Island Guest Services
1.800.234.1666

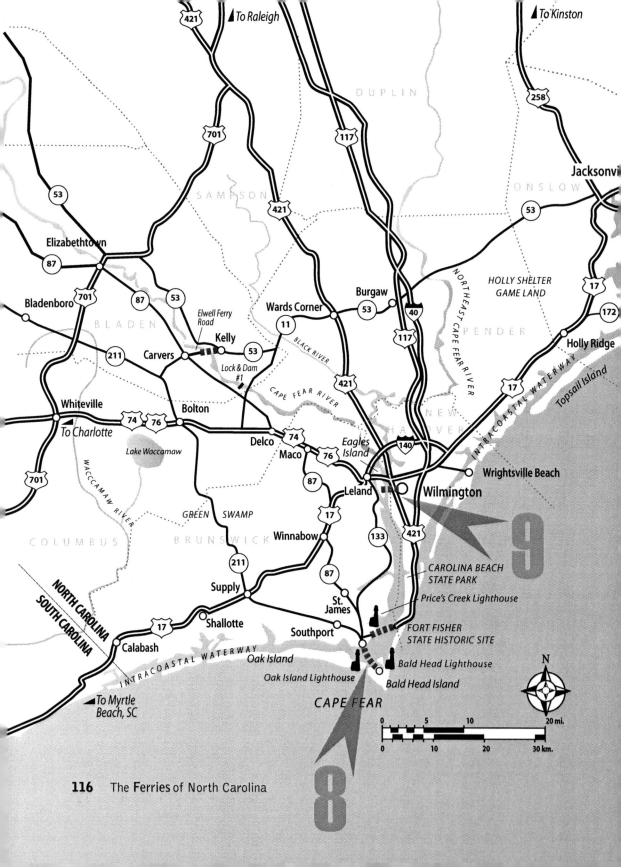

To Raleigh

To Kinston

421

258

DUPLIN

701

117

53

Jacksonvi

ONSLOW

SAMPSON

421

53

Elizabethtown

87

HOLLY SHELTER
GAME LAND

Burgaw

Bladenboro

701

87

53

Wards Corner

53

40

17

PENDER

Elwell Ferry
Road

11

117

172

Carvers

Kelly

53

BLACK RIVER

Holly Ridge

211

Lock & Dam
#1

CAPE FEAR RIVER

421

NORTHEAST CAPE FEAR RIVER

17

INTRACOASTAL WATERWAY

Topsail Island

Whiteville

74

76

Bolton

To Charlotte

Delco

74

Maco

Eagles
Island

140

NEW HANOVER

Lake Waccamaw

76

87

Leland

Wrightsville Beach

Wilmington

701

WACCAMAW RIVER

GREEN SWAMP

17

421

COLUMBUS

BRUNSWICK

Winnabow

133

9

211

CAROLINA BEACH
STATE PARK

87

Supply

Price's Creek Lighthouse

NORTH CAROLINA
SOUTH CAROLINA

Shallotte

St.
James

FORT FISHER
STATE HISTORIC SITE

17

Calabash

Southport

Bald Head Lighthouse

INTRACOASTAL WATERWAY

Oak Island

Oak Island Lighthouse

Bald Head Island

To Myrtle
Beach, SC

CAPE FEAR

N

0   5   10   20 mi.

0   10   20   30 km.

8

116   The **Ferries** of North Carolina

Bald Head Island GETTING THERE

Wilmington, NC, to Bald Head Island (Indigo) ferry landing

From downtown Wilmington, take US74 W / US76 W west across the Cape Fear Memorial Bridge, for 2.7 miles. At the first exit, take the NC133 S ramp 0.3 miles toward Southport / Oak Island. Turn left onto NC 133 / Village Rd. NE. Proceed 22.6 miles. At the intersection, stay straight to go onto NC87 / River Rd. SE Continue 1.2 miles until you get to traffic light at NC 211. (For shopping on Long Beach Road, take a right here.)

Turn left onto NC 211 / N. Howe St. for Southport riverfront and the ferry landings. You'll see the NC Ferries schedule posted and know you're on the right track. Go .7 mile the second traffic light (W. 9th St.), and turn right for the Bald Head Island ferry. From the traffic light it's 1.4 miles further to the ferry. The road will take you through a residential area and a school zone, where you'll make a hard left and come to the Indigo Landing development.

Proceed through the white gates, making a right turn and continuing past the Bald Head Island remote parking lots. Visitors may park in lots B, C, or D on a space available basis; a shuttle runs a regular circuit to the ferry landing.

Total est. distance: 29 miles
Total est. time: 45 minutes

From US 17 in Shallotte, NC, and points south (Myrtle Beach, SC) to Bald Head Island (Indigo) ferry landing

Proceed north on US 17 N / Ocean Hwy. Seven miles north of Shallotte, turn right on NC 211 / Southport-Supply Rd.; continue 16.3 miles to the second traffic light (W. 9th St.). Turn right for the Bald Head Island ferry. From the traffic light it's 1.4 miles further to the ferry. The road will take you through a residential area and a school zone, where you'll make a hard left and come to the Indigo Landing development.

Proceed through the white gates, making a right turn and continuing past the Bald Head Island remote parking lots. Visitors may park in lots B, C, or D on a space available basis; a shuttle runs a regular circuit to the ferry landing.

Total est. distance: 24 miles
Total est. time: 35 minutes

On Bald Head Island

The ferry dock is located at the Bald Head Island Marina. Allow plenty of time for tram transportation from your lodgings (the far end of the island is a 20-minute drive by tram), or to return your rented golf cart to Island Passage.

Wilmington Eagles Island SCHEDULE

GETTING THERE

Map, p. 116

Departs Riverfront Park (Wilmington)	Departs Battleship Park (Eagles Island)
Summer Schedule MEMORIAL DAY–LABOR DAY	
10.00 am	---
---	10.15 am
From Memorial Day to Labor Day, the water taxi operates daily from 10 am to 5 pm, except 11 am and 3 pm, when sightseeing tours are in progress.	
---	4.45 pm
5.00 pm	---
	5.15 pm

Departs Riverfront Park (Wilmington)	Departs Battleship Park (Eagles Island)
Spring and Fall Schedule APRIL–MAY SEPTEMBER–OCTOBER WEEKENDS ONLY	
10.00 am	---
---	10.15 am
From early April until Memorial Day, and Labor Day through the end of October, the water taxi operates Saturday and Sunday from 10 am to 5 pm, except 11 am and 3 pm, when sightseeing tours are in progress.	
---	4.45 pm
11.00 pm	---
	5.15 pm

Wilmington's Riverfront Park is located at the foot of Market St. at its intersection with Water St. Metered streetfront parking is available nearby; city parking garages are located within three blocks.

Wilmington's riverfront features hardly more tall buildings than it did a century ago.

CHAPTER **9** # Wilmington Eagles Island

passenger-only ferry

route Crosses the Cape Fear River from downtown Wilmington (pop. 91,137, New Hanover County) to Eagles Island (Brunswick County)

duration 20 min round trip

distance 200 yards across

vessel and capacity 50' launch; 48 passengers

fare Adults $3 Children under 2 free

reservations Not required

schedule Departs Riverfront Park on the quarter hour; departs Battleship Park on the hour and half hour except 11.00 am and 3.00 pm, seasonally

terminal Riverfront Park, Market and Water Streets, Wilmington NC 28401

information 1.800.676.0162; 910.343.1611 **Web** www.cfrboats.com/ watertaxi.html

shore facilities Riverfront Park: visitor center; restrooms; proximity to downtown Wilmington amenities Battleship Park: Tours with paid admission; gift shop and canteen; restrooms; covered picnic area

WILMINGTON'S MOST FAMOUS BOAT DOESN'T *actually go anywhere anymore—she is, of course, the Showboat, the USS* North Carolina *that's been berthed permanently at Eagles Island in the Cape Fear River since 1961. "The Battleship," as everyone around here knows her, is one of the Port City's most recognizable landmarks and popular tourist attractions. It's only appropriate that visitors can reach her by boat.*

The Captain J. N. Maffitt, *a former Navy launch refitted as a water taxi and excursion boat, plies the waters between downtown Wilmington's Riverfront Park and the Battleship landing daily each hour. Sure, you can drive around by way of the Cape Fear Memorial Bridge or the Isabel Holmes Bridge—but the water taxi provides a perspective on the giant battleship that visitors arriving by land don't get.*

Or, if you're not keen on searching for a parking place while visiting Wilmington's riverfront attractions, you can always

The Coast Guard tall ship *Eagle,* making a rare call at the port of Wilmington

park at Eagles Island, tour the Battleship, and take the taxi across to see a bit of downtown. Either way, the twenty-minute harbor tour (ten minutes each way) lets you take in sights from bridge to bridge.

The Captain Maffitt *is named for Wilmington legend Capt. John Newland Maffitt, the "High Seas Confederate" who resigned his U.S. Navy commission at the outset of the War between the States and took command of the CSS* Florida. *The original Capt. Maffitt*

plagued Union shipping throughout the conflict. His namesake boat was put into service in Wilmington in 1978.

Passengers departing from either side may disembark and obtain a pass for the return portion of their trip, good on any later crossing. Sightseeing cruises on the Cape Fear River and scenic tours of the Northeast Cape Fear River are also scheduled regularly.

WILMINGTON, AN IMPORTANT port during colonial and revolutionary times, a strategic location during the Civil War, and a vital shipbuilding center during the first and second World Wars, is situated twenty miles up the Cape Fear River from the Atlantic Ocean. The city's distance from the sea afforded it protection, while its isolation from other urban areas restricted major industrial and residential development until well into the twentieth century.

Those days are no more—Wilmington and its surrounding counties in southeastern North Carolina are experiencing record growth as newcomers discover the region's natural beauty, history, and resources. The film industry also discovered Wilmington in the mid-1980s, so it's not unusual to spot actors and directors around town or to happen upon a movie or TV shoot in progress.

Much of Wilmington's appeal has to do with its proximity to water—the Cape Fear River to the west, and the Intracoastal Waterway and the Atlantic Ocean eight miles to the east. Its beaches have long been desirable vacation and second-home destinations.

So it's only natural that Wilmington should have a fair share of nautical recreations. Downtown, in addition to the Battleship and the water taxi, there's the riverboat *Henrietta III,* which offers regular sightseeing and dinner cruises. The Coast Guard cutter *Diligence,* docked on the riverfront, is open to tours on special occasions.

At Wrightsville Beach, water taxi services may shuttle patrons to "dock and dine" restaurants and other locations (such as the private Figure Eight Island), and a sunset cruise departs from Banks Channel in front of the Blockade Runner resort. On occasion charter service is available to the Masonboro Island nature preserve, though there is no regularly scheduled water taxi at present.

Accommodations, dining, and **recreation** are abundant in Wilmington—the downtown historic district boasts numerous B&Bs as well as a high-rise Hilton, and between downtown and the beach almost all of the major chain motels are represented. Superb restaurants are located only a few steps from Riverfront Park; two blocks' walk will also take you to the Dixie Grill for breakfast or the Trolly Stop for a classic hot dog.

Wilmington's historic Thalian Hall theatre is only one of many performing arts venues located downtown. For more unusual amusements, visit the Cape Fear Serpentarium on Dock Street, join up with the Haunted Pub Crawl, take a trolley or horse-drawn carriage tour and see how many film locations or celebrities you can spot, or stop in at your choice of tattoo parlors. (Some things in port towns never change.)

Other guidebooks have covered Wilmington's tourist scene at great length (I especially recommend the *Insiders' Guide*)—so this list won't attempt to duplicate them.

Wrightsville Beach is minutes from downtown.

But if you're in downtown Wilmington to ride the *Captain Maffitt* and have time for only one further diversion, be sure to sign up for the Wilmington Adventure Tours hosted by guide extraordinaire Bob Jenkins. You'll find information at the Riverfront Park—and you'll know Bob by his hat and walking stick.

At the Two Sisters Bookery in the Cotton Exchange, you'll find lots to read about Wilmington history and culture. My particular favorites for good local stories, however, are Philip Gerard's historical novel *Cape Fear Rising* (1997), Danny Bradshaw's *Ghosts on the Battleship North Carolina* (2002), and Cindy Horrell Ramsey's *The Boys of the Battleship* (2007).

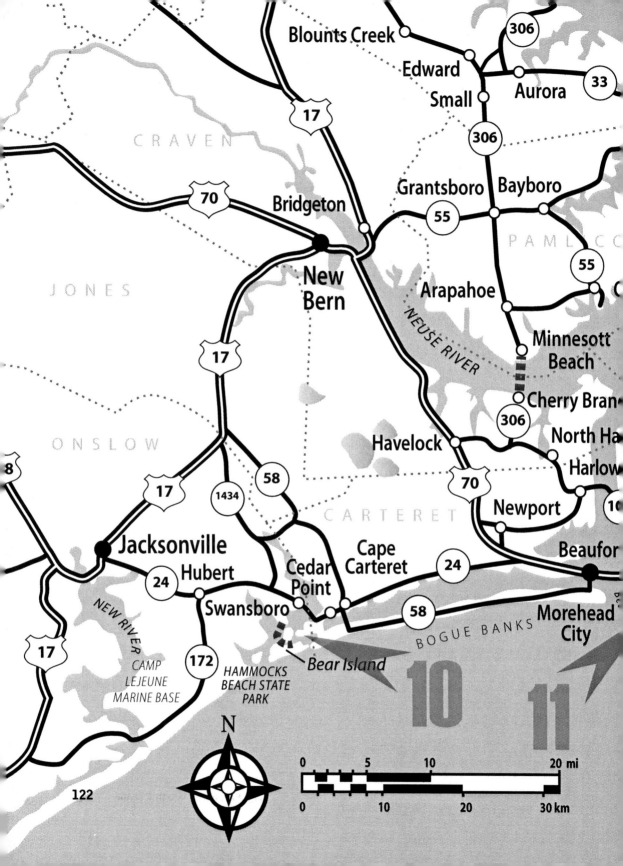

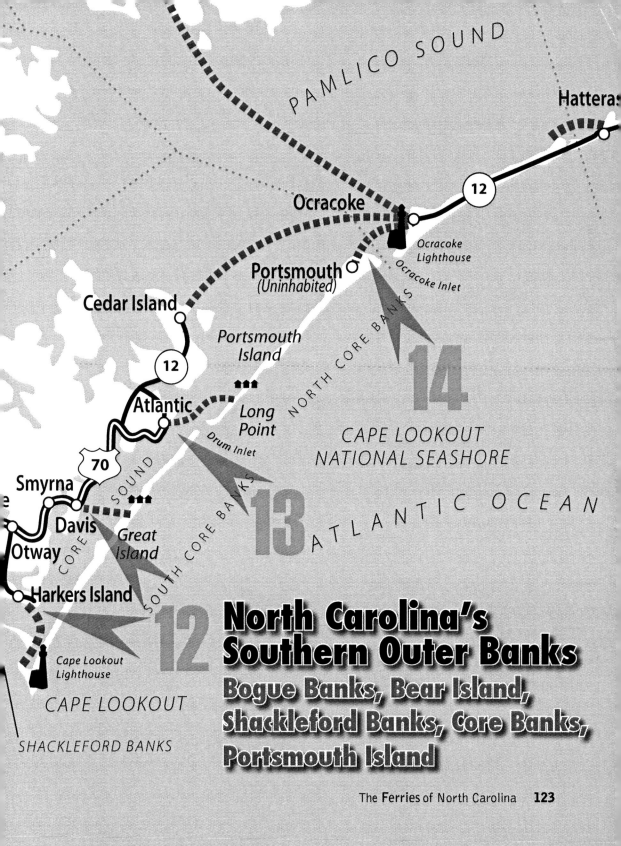

PAMLICO SOUND

Hatteras

12

Ocracoke

Ocracoke
Lighthouse

Ocracoke Inlet

Portsmouth
(Uninhabited)

Cedar Island

12

*Portsmouth
Island*

NORTH CORE BANKS

14

Atlantic

*Long
Point*

Drum Inlet

CAPE LOOKOUT
NATIONAL SEASHORE

ATLANTIC OCEAN

70

Smyrna

CORE SOUND

SOUTH CORE BANKS

13

Davis

*Great
Island*

Otway

CORE

Harkers Island

SOUTH CORE BANKS

12

*Cape Lookout
Lighthouse*

CAPE LOOKOUT

SHACKLEFORD BANKS

North Carolina's
Southern Outer Banks
Bogue Banks, Bear Island,
Shackleford Banks, Core Banks,
Portsmouth Island

Hammocks Beach State Park FERRY SCHEDULE

GETTING THERE
Map, pp. 122–23

Jacksonville, NC, to Hammocks Beach State Park
From downtown Jacksonville, follow NC 24 / Lejeune Blvd. east for 15.4 miles. Turn right at Hammocks Beach Rd. (by the ABC store before the first Swansboro traffic light). Proceed 2.1 miles south to the park entrance, which is on the right. The visitor center is 0.2 miles, at the end of the road.
Total est. distance: 17.7 miles
Total est. time: 30 minutes

Morehead City, NC, to Hammocks Beach State Park
From downtown Morehead City, follow US 70 / Arendell St. west for 4 miles. Bear left onto NC 24; proceed west for 21 miles, through Cape Carteret, across the White Oak River causeway and bridge, and through Swansboro. Turn left on Hammocks Beach Rd., just past the last Swansboro traffic light. Proceed 2.1 miles south to the park entrance, which is on the right. The visitor center is 0.2 miles, at the end of the road.
Total est. distance: 27.3 miles
Total est. time: 40 minutes

Shoulder Season

Departs Park Headquarters	Departs Bear Island
MAY AND SEPTEMBER WEDNESDAY–SUNDAY	
9.30 am	10.00 am
10.30 am	11.00 am
11.30 am	12.00 noon
12.30 pm	1.00 pm
1.30 pm	2.00 pm
2.30 pm	3.00 pm
3.30 pm	4.00 pm
4.30 pm	5.00 pm

Off Season

Departs Park Headquarters	Departs Bear Island
APRIL AND OCTOBER FRIDAY–SUNDAY	
9.30 am	10.00 am
10.30 am	11.00 am
11.30 am	12.00 noon
12.30 pm	1.00 pm
1.30 pm	2.00 pm
2.30 pm	3.00 pm
3.30 pm	4.00 pm
4.30 pm	5.00 pm

High Season

Departs Park Headquarters	Departs Bear Island	Departs Park Headquarters	Departs Bear Island
MEMORIAL DAY– LABOR DAY MONDAY AND TUESDAY		MEMORIAL DAY– LABOR DAY WEDNESDAY–SUNDAY	
9.30 am	10.00 am	9.30 am	10.00 am
10.30 am	11.00 am	10.00 am	10.30 am
11.30 am	12.00 noon	10.30 am	11.00 am
12.30 pm	1.00 pm	11.00 am	11.30 am
1.30 pm	2.00 pm	11.30 am	12.00 noon
2.30 pm	3.00 pm	12.00 noon	12.30 pm
3.30 pm	4.00 pm	12.30 pm	1.00 pm
4.30 pm	5.00 pm	1.00 pm	1.30 pm
5.30 pm	6.00 pm	1.30 pm	2.00 pm
		2.00 pm	2.30 pm
		2.30 pm	3.00 pm
		3.00 pm	3.30 pm
		3.30 pm	4.00 pm
		4.00 pm	4.30 pm
		4.30 pm	5.00 pm
		5.00 pm	5.30 pm
		5.30 pm	6.00 pm

10 Hammocks Beach State Park Bear Island

passenger-only ferry, seasonal

route Crosses Intracoastal Waterway and Cow Channel from Hammocks Beach Rd., off NC Hwy. 24 near town of **Swansboro** (pop. 1,334, Onslow County) to **Hammocks Beach State Park**, Onslow County

duration 25 min

distance 2.5 mi

vessels and capacity
24′ skiffs, 11 passengers
40′ pontoon boats, 28 passengers

fare $5

reservations Not available

schedule
Hourly 9.30 am–5 pm selected days
April–October;
additional crossings in summer

terminal
1572 Hammocks Beach Rd.,
Swansboro NC 28584

information
910.326.4881
hammocks.beach@ncmail.net
Web www.ils.unc.edu/parkproject/visit/
habe/home.html

terminal/shore facilities Mainland: Interpretive center/park office, restrooms, vending machines, gazebo and picnic tables, canoe/kayak launch Bear Island: Concession stand, restrooms/bathhouse, water (seasonally), primitive camping

FOLKS WHO HAVE SPENT ANY TIME ON *the coast know that the day after a hurricane is a mixture of beauty and destruction. This morning, only hours after Hurricane Isabel's 85-mile-an-hour winds brushed this barrier island, visitors on the ferry don't know which to expect. The cool September sky sparkles, the water is clear and calm, the*

Once you step off the ferry on Bear Island, white-sand beaches are only a fifteen-minute walk away.

marsh grass and scrub cedar are fragrant and fresh after the night's deluge.

The pontoon boat carries a full load: a group of students from Chapel Hill who drove all night in the rain, determined to go ahead with their weekend camping trip; a family with small kids, eager to enjoy one last day at the beach before it gets too cold to swim; a few anxious park personnel. They have all heard the news reports by now—that Isabel's most powerful wrath has hit north of here, where it has devastated homes, roads, and utilities and carved a new inlet on Hatteras Island.

Hammocks Beach, though, has been spared the worst. Its brand-new concession stand, restroom facilities, and picnic shelters will open as scheduled today. The beaches are smooth and inviting. The ferry will run. Life goes on.

HAMMOCKS BEACH STATE PARK is a paradise for those who enjoy sun and sand and gentle waters. While accessible only by boat, it's closer to the mainland and to urban areas than the Outer Banks, and it also benefits from its more sheltered, southeast-facing location.

The park consists of an interpretive center and ferry landing situated on 33 acres on the mainland, and the 892-acre Bear Island. Lush cordgrass marsh characterizes the western (sound) side of the island, while dramatic white beach strand marks the eastern (Atlantic Ocean) side. Small boats must navigate a network of shallow waterways with extreme care to reach the dock on the island.

Bear Island was once part of the hunting grounds of the Tuscarora Indians. Its current name results from a misspelling, when surveyors back in the days of cattle grazing erroneously transcribed maps of "Bare Is-

land." Today the island's high dunes support a diversity of vegetation, from goldenrod, sea oats, and beachgrass to upland tree species such as loblolly pine, red cedar, oak, and red bay. Among its significant animal species is the loggerhead turtle, which nests here undisturbed by roads, vehicles, or human habitation.

The property, which had been used for military defense at times up through the Civil War, was purchased in the early twentieth century by Dr. William Sharpe of New York as a hunting preserve. At the suggestion of his longtime hunting guide and friend John Hurst, in 1950 Sharpe deeded the island to the North Carolina Teachers Association, an organization of African American educators.

Hammocks Beach's fourteen campsites are situated among the dunes.

It was eventually acquired by the state of North Carolina and opened as a state park in 1961.

Hammocks Beach has become a popular location for camping, swimming, fishing, canoeing, and kayaking, serving nearly 134,000 visitors in 2005. Facilities on the island are

onsite; there is an emergency phone located at the concession stand on the island.

There are two ways to reach Bear Island: by private boat (or canoe or kayak), or by the park-operated ferry. Ferry service is first come, first served, morning to late afternoon, April through October; during shoulder seasons the ferry may run only on selected days.

If you're headed to the beach for an overnight stay, don't figure on one of those large ferryboats that ply the sounds north of here. Due to shallow channels and severe shoaling on this short route, operators use either a 40-foot pontoon boat or an even smaller 24-foot skiff to transport visitors and their gear. Consequently, there are strict limits on what can be carried aboard—no wagons or carts, for instance (two-wheeled coolers are okay).

The 40-foot pontoon boat (top) that provides ferry service to Hammocks Beach is supplemented by flat-bottomed skiffs (below) for traversing the shallow waters of Cow Channel during low tides.

limited, however, and all gear must be carried from the dock area across the dunes to campsites, a good fifteen-minute walk.

Reservations are required for the fourteen oceanfront campsites and the group camp. Camping is permitted year-round, though fresh water is available only seasonally. No campfires are allowed on the island. After hours, there are no park personnel

"We encourage campers to think of this as primitive backpack camping," says ranger Paul Donnelly. "Whatever you can pack in your backpack, take half of that out and leave it home. What you can carry on your back, you can bring aboard the ferry." Check the park's website for more details.

Donnelly also reminds campers that they are allowed one free trip back to the mainland each day for ice and supplies, with proof

The **Ferries** of North Carolina   **127**

of camping registration. A ferry ticket must be obtained at the visitor center for each round trip.

You'll want to get to park headquarters early to avoid long lines during periods of heavy demand. Be aware that the ferry schedule can be unexpectedly interrupted at low tide.

But while you wait, you can take advantage of the fascinating nature and history exhibits in the visitor center. Rangers hold regularly scheduled interpretive programs throughout the summer; environmental

Hammocks Beach State Park is a secluded paradise accessible only by boat.

education activities are also available for teachers and their students.

The visitor center is open 8 am–6 pm June through August and 8 am to 5 pm September through May (closed Christmas Day). Ample parking and shaded areas for picnicking are provided, as are restrooms, vending machines, and pay phone. For canoeists and kayakers headed out on the desig-

nated paddle trails SC-ON-1 and SC-ON-2, there is an excellent over-the-water launch pad onsite. Consult North Carolina Coastal Paddle Trails at www.ncsu.edu/paddletrails for maps, ratings, and helpful advice.

•

Swansboro, five minutes away, is the nearest municipality. This small port town dates to colonial days, when Capt. Otway Burns was the most well-known privateer in these parts. It hasn't lost its quaint waterfront charm, even though jets from nearby military bases fly overhead and beach-bound traffic rushes by on NC Highway 24. Lining the narrow streets of Swansboro you'll find comfortable cafés and seafood restaurants, a coffeehouse, and a slew of boutiques, galleries, and antiques stores. **Accommodations** include a couple of B&Bs and an independent motel in Swansboro, as well as a few motels across the river in Cedar Point (the Best Western Silver Creek is particularly handy). Further along NC 58 on the mainland are numerous motels and RV resorts, while on the Bogue Banks the Emerald Coast beach towns offer lots of choices.

The Ace Hardware and Western Auto

stores in this vicinity offer far more than nuts and bolts: they're great places to find equipment for your Hammocks Beach trip (don't forget extra-long tent stakes), or a repair part for your boat, or a bit of friendly advice or directions.

Swansboro has a small grocery store, and there is a convenience store with gas and a bank ATM at the turnoff for Hammocks Beach Road.

•

Jacksonville, since 1941 home of Camp Lejeune Marine Corps Base, is a city of 66,000—61% male, median age 22, if that tells you anything. The establishment of the Marine Corps base and the Marine Corps Air Station New River have brought booming population growth to the area. But you can dine economically on virtually any world cuisine you desire, get a tattoo or a high-and-tight buzz cut, pawn your guitar, or purchase an affordable mobile home or used car. Or obtain anything you might need 24/7 in the way of supplies, groceries, gas, auto repair, or overnight accommodations. It's a 30-minute drive west on NC 24 from Hammocks Beach State Park.

Another nearby town—about an hour east of the park—is **Morehead City**. See chapter 12 for more on Morehead.

For more information
• Jacksonville-Onslow Chamber of Commerce, www.jacksonvilleonline.com 910.347.3141
• Swansboro Chamber of Commerce, www.swansboronccchamber.com 910.326.1174

Ghost crabs quickly retreat beneath the sand.

The ferry dock on the mainland provides a peaceful view of the waterway—and shelter if you have to wait.

Cape Lookout National Seashore / Shackleford Banks FERRY SCHEDULES

GETTING THERE

Map, pp. 122–23

Departs Beaufort/ Morehead City Mainland	Departs Shackleford Banks
Seasonal or year-round schedules	
first departure 8.00 am	---
---	first return 8.30 am
Ferry schedules vary, but generally depart as early as 8 am and return as late as 5.30 pm, seven days a week, according to demand	
last departure 5.00 pm	
---	last return 5.30 pm

New Bern, NC, to Beaufort waterfront
From downtown New Bern, take US 70 E in a southerly direction across either of the Trent River bridges. Proceed 40 miles, through the towns of Havelock, Newport, and Morehead City across the bridges into Beaufort. In downtown Beaufort, take any right turn off US 70 / Cedar St. on a through street 3 blocks to Front St. Ferry services will be located at various points harborside.
Total est. distance: 41 miles
Total est. time: 1 hour

Jacksonville, NC, to Beaufort waterfront
From downtown Jacksonville, take NC 24 E in a southerly direction 37 miles, through the towns of Swansboro, Cape Carteret, and Bogue to the intersection with US 70. Bear right (east) and proceed 8 miles through Morehead City and across the bridges into Beaufort. In downtown Beaufort, take any right turn off US 70 / Arendell St. on a through street 3 blocks to Front St. Ferry services will be located at various points harborside.
Total est. distance: 45 miles
Total est. time: 1 hour

Cedar Island, NC, to Beaufort waterfront
From the ferry landing at Cedar Island, take NC 12 for 12 miles west, past the Atlantic turnoff, to US 70 W. Proceed 20.7 miles, turning at intersections as necessary to remain on US 70. In the community of North River Center, turn left (south) on US 70 / Live Oak St. Proceed 5.2 miles to downtown Beaufort; turn right (west) on Cedar St. Take any right turn off US 70 / Cedar St. on a through street 3 blocks to Front St. Ferry services will be located at various points harborside.
Total est. distance: 38 miles
Total est. time: 1 hour

CHAPTER 11

Cape Lookout National Seashore Shackleford Banks

passenger-only ferries

routes Cross Taylors Creek, Back Sound, and adjacent waters from **Morehead City** (pop. 8,485, Carteret County) or town of **Beaufort** (pop. 4,000) to Shackleford Banks and nearby islands (Carteret County)

duration 5 to 45 min

distance 0.25 mi to Carrot Island
5 mi to Shackleford Banks

vessels, capacity, fare, schedule
Vary according to destination, season, and day of week

reservations
Highly recommended, though many services have walk-up ticket booths dockside

terminal, shore facilities
Ferry landings at Morehead City waterfront, Beaufort waterfront; also at Harkers Island; facilities vary

information
A helpful, updated summary of authorized ferry services is found on the Cape Lookout Natitonal Seashore website at www.nps.gov/calo/ferry.htm

THE FERRY LANDING—IF YOU CAN CALL IT *that—is a twenty-foot-wide stretch of beach between two sign-posts. But when we hop off the skiff onto the sand, we're within a few hundred yards of some of the best tidal-pool swimming, shell hunting, and bird watching on the East Coast. The waters of the sound are calm and blue, the sky a brilliant turquoise. A*

Wild ponies have been part of the Shackleford Banks landscape for hundreds of years; today they are federally protected and are identified for study and management.

half-mile hike to the south, and we come upon a pair of shaggy-maned ponies grazing between the dunes.

This is Shackleford Banks, a study in contrasts. The wildest of North Carolina's national-seashore islands, it's within easy view of the seaport at Morehead City. An island devoid of human habitation today, in the 1800s it supported a thriving fishing and whaling community called Diamond City. Its east–west orientation encourages development of tall dunes, and its diverse habitats range from maritime forest to tidal marsh to broad beach strand.

At this latitude, traveling due east would take you eventually to the coast of Morocco, somewhere around Casablanca. The seclusion of this rugged barrier island makes it seem almost as exotic as a faraway land.

THE TRIO OF NARROW BARRIER islands forming a large check-mark off the coast of Carteret County between Beaufort Inlet and Ocracoke Inlet, collectively known as the Southern Outer Banks and protected since 1966 as the Cape Lookout National Seashore, offers some of the last truly primi-

The landing on Shackleford Banks

tive beachfront in the state and some of the most fascinating chapters of its history.

And there is good reason: the isolation that defined the region's natural, economic, and social history continues today, as the islands are accessible only by water. Though the Shackleford Banks and the North and South Core Banks are popular destinations for private boaters, sea-kayakers, and canoeists, numerous ferry services provide transportation and tours. Some of these also operate official cabin concessions for the National Park Service, providing minimal overnight accommodations on North and South Core Banks.

A brief lesson on the area's unique **geology and geography** will help newcomers get a sense of what to expect. According to naturalist Dirk Frankenberg, whose 1997 book *North Carolina's Southern Coast: Barrier Islands, Coastal Waters, and Wetlands* goes into great depth on these matters, variables such as the location of ancient shorelines and the effects of current-day tidal range determine whether a particular stretch of coastal topgraphy will be flat and subject to frequent overwash, or more elevated and tending to form a web of small islands and tidal inlets.

North Carolina's long, thin, sandy, low-lying barrier islands—from Shackleford at the southern extreme to Currituck at the northern end—are prime examples of the former instance. They feature few navigable inlets to the sea—but during storms the forces of wind and water always threaten to shoal up existing channels or cut new ones. Owing to their ever-shifting nature they pose challenges to human occupation, and they are more accurately called *banks* than islands. Shifting sands also build bars for many miles out to sea, presenting challenges to oceangoing vessels. A recent *National Geographic* map plots more than 500 shipwrecks from Cape Lookout to Cape Henry, in Virginia.

Shackleford, which faces south rather than taking the brunt of the Atlantic head-on, has developed and retained more stable vegetation than most of the other banks (though its grass cover was severely threatened by overgrazing of livestock until the National Park Service began to remove animals in the 1940s). It is separated from Cape Lookout and the South Core Banks by Beaufort Inlet, a deep-water inlet since at least the early 1700s.

The Core Banks, which face in a southeasterly direction, have been more or less contiguous over time—these narrow land masses are like long beads on a necklace, sometimes drifting together, sometimes shifting apart.

At present, Core Banks is divided into two sections at about 34°51' north latitude by manmade Drum Inlet, so there is no access from one stretch to the other. North Core Banks is periodically further broken up by swashes and flooded tidal flats. Over the years maps, signs, and accounts have attached varying labels to the resulting "islands": zoom in close on Google Earth and you'll spot names seen in few guidebooks today. Although there is no true Great Island, and Portsmouth Island is technically part and parcel of North Core Banks, you will certainly benefit by knowing where these are

Kayaking is popular on the in-shore waters between the mainland and Cape Lookout.

located.

And since the Cape Lookout National Seashore comprises such a long stretch—56 miles of oceanfront—it's essential to know just where along this slender thread you want the ferry to deposit you. The Park Service provides maps with mile markers noted north to south. Study up and decide ahead of time whether you want to reserve a cabin and do some surf fishing, or take a walking tour through historic Portsmouth Village, or surf at the Cape Lookout Lighthouse, and that's how you'll determine the right ferry to take you there.

Driving is permitted on North and South Core Banks, if you have the right vehicle (four-wheel-drive or all-terrain vehicle), the expertise to drive it on sand, and an arrangement with a ferry service to transport it over and back. (More about beach driving in chapter 13.) Due to recent increases in ATV use, the National Part Service has begun reminding visitors that ATVs are sanctioned for transportation, not recreation—the Banks are a fragile ecosystem not suited for off-road sports. No motorized vehicles are allowed on Shackleford Banks. Bicycles are allowed throughout the Seashore.

The extent of **preparations** you will need to make depends on how long you intend to stay on the islands. Regardless where you go on the national seashore, sufficient drinking water and food must be carried with you, and all trash must be carried out. As noted earlier, configurations of the ferryboats that serve these routes vary widely. You can board the 149-passenger speedboat *Lookout Express* for a day's exploration of Cape Lookout, or you can arrange for the ferry service at Davis to haul you and all your gear *and* your 4WD Jeep over to Great Island on the Core Banks.

Local information can and does change frequently—such as when storms like 2003's Hurricane Isabel altered the islands' topography, accelerated shoaling in boat channels, and even put some tourist enterprises and lodgings out of business.

Fare and schedule information listed in these sections is subject to change; consult the park service's list of approved concessions on page 139 or check the park's website for an updated list. (In general, costs range from $10 and up per adult, round trip, to $65 and up for a vehicle.) Also, rules regarding pets and leash requirements differ according to service and destination; check first. Detailed information regarding access, overnight camping, and beach safety is available on the national seashore's website at www.nps.gov/calo.

•

Shackleford Banks, the 2,500-acre, 9-mile-long island forming the short arm of the check-mark, is deserted today—except for the wild Banker ponies and other nonhuman inhabitants. The great hurricane of 1899 devastated the island, leveling the cluster of homes and the high dunes that once protected them, and surviving residents resettled at Harkers Island or the "Promise' Land" of Morehead City. Visitors to Shackleford Banks today can watch the free-roaming bands of ponies, whose origin is uncertain but which may have been related to Spanish shipwrecks in the 1500s, or they can explore the island's ghost forests or the site of Diamond City.

Be advised that the ferry services from Beaufort drop off passengers at the dock on the far western end of the island, on the opposite end eight miles from Diamond City, and hiking in deep or wet sand can take some effort. Ferries from Harkers Island provide access to the eastern end of "Shack" and to the Cape Lookout Lighthouse, which is situated across a 300-yard-wide inlet on a different island.

The Banks **beaches** are legendary for seashells (but don't remove any live specimens). The shallow waters of the sound side are hospitable for canoeing, kayaking, scuba diving, and swimming. The ocean side can be risky for swimmers, especially as there are no lifeguards on any of the beaches. Lots of folks come to these waters to fish, and in the fall, hunting season is open for waterfowl.

The National Park Service organizes programs for watching **horses** on Shackleford Banks throughout the summer months.

Departure locations and times vary; the Park Service will make your ferry arrangements for you and provide directions. (Even

The federally protected ponies are identified for study and management.

if you take your own boat, you'll need a Park Service reservation to participate.) Call 252.728.2250 x 3002.

•

The ferry services can also carry you to several other small islands. Services from Morehead City can schedule trips to **Sugarloaf Island, Sand Dollar Island,** and **Bird Shoal.** A five-minute boat ride from Beaufort, **Carrot Island** and the **Rachel Carson Coastal Reserve,** an estuarine island dense with vegetation and bird life, are open to serious naturalists and researchers. Wild ponies roam Carrot Island, and its proximity to the mainland attracts kayakers to come in for a

closer view as well. More information about the reserve is available at www.ncnerr.org.

•

On the mainland, **Morehead City** is a major port for commercial shipping, commercial fishing, charter fishing, and recreational boating. It is also headquarters of the North Carolina Ferry Division (which is open to the public only by appointment). Morehead City's attractive waterfront welcomes visitors by land and sea with excellent seafood dining, cafes, and boutiques.

Accommodations, dining, groceries, gas, and provisions are plentiful in town and on the Crystal Coast beaches. Chain and independent hotels and motels, B&Bs and inns, and private campgrounds welcome the traveler headed for the southern Outer Banks—still, an affordable bed for one or two nights can be hard to come by. In beach season or fishing season, it's best to have a reservation.

The North Carolina Aquarium at Pine Knoll Shores has been recently renovated and was reopened to eager visitors in May 2006. The Fort Macon State Historic Site—the most popular of North Carolina's historic sites—hosts Civil War reenactments on a regular basis.

Across the Intracoastal Waterway is the historic county seat of **Beaufort** (BO-fort, unlike the South Carolina town, BEW-fort), a longtime magnet for mariners, and the site of the North Carolina Maritime Museum. Beaufort is the gateway to the Down East

Ferries depart from the Beaufort waterfront.

tends toward trendy boutiques or vintage downtown stores; for big-box discount stores or 24-hour groceries, head over the bridge to Morehead City.

For **fun,** Beaufort offers plenty to do day and night. The Ghost Walk tour is popular, here in Blackbeard's old stomping ground; you can also take part in a guided walking or bus tour. Dinner and sunset cruises can be reserved at the excursion-boat offices on the waterfront—just about every water sport or coastal-recreation activity you can imagine is within reach here. But if you're stuck on land, don't miss the fascinating North Carolina Maritime Museum, right there on Front Street.

•

If you're interested in **reading** more about Carteret County and Down East, a wealth of historical fact and fiction awaits you. Bland Simpson beautifully evokes the spirit of the region with his wife, Ann Cary Simpson, in the "Haystacks" chapter of *Into the Sound Country: A Carolinian's Coastal Plain* (1997)—and go ahead and read the rest of the book while you're at it. Lynn Salsi and Frances Eubanks's volumes in the Arcadia Images of America series—*Carteret County* (1999) and *Voices of the Crystal*

communities of Harkers Island, Davis, and Atlantic (see chapter 13), where ferries provide access to other parts of the Cape Lookout National Seashore. US 70 E from Beaufort is also the lone route to the Outer Banks ferry landing at Cedar Island (see chapter 4).

Beaufort is practically awash in charming **inns and B&Bs,** many located in the historic district, where homes date back to the 1700s. **Dining choices** range from sandwich shops and seafood restaurants along Front Street, to barbecue to Italian to pub grub. (For a seaport treat, order up a Dark & Stormy, a concoction of ginger beer and dark rum.) Beaufort's reputation as a regional epicurean center is underscored by an annual slate of festivals and food events. **Shopping**

Coast (2000) — provide historical information. B. J. Mountford, following her earlier novel set in Portsmouth Village, published *Bloodlines of Shackleford Banks: A Mystery* in 2004.

For more information
• Carteret County Tourism Development Authority, www.sunnync.com, 1.800.SUNNY-NC / 1.880.786.6962 or 252.726.8148
• Carteret County Chamber of Commerce, 252.726.6350
• Cape Lookout National Seashore, National Park Service, Harkers Island, NC, www.nps.gov/calo

MOREHEAD CITY
Morehead City's municipal docks may be reached by turning south off US 70 / Arendell St. at 10th St. City parking is readily available, and a café is located close to the dock.

Sugarloaf Island Ferry Service
carries passengers to a 47-acre undeveloped island within sight of downtown Morehead City popular for its walking trails and sandy beaches.

10th and Shepherd Sts., Morehead City NC 28557
$8 adults / $6 seniors / $4 children 11 and under; call for schedule and reservations.
252.726.7678

Waterfront Ferry Service ferries passengers from the dock beside the State Port office to brief visits to Sand Dollar Island, Bird Shoal, and Carrot Island, all within sight distance of Beaufort.

Portside Marina
209 Arendell St., Morehead City, NC 28557
$12 adults / $6 ages 12 and under
Minimum trip $48
1.877.434.7678
252.726.7678

BEAUFORT
Beaufort's city docks and ferry services stretch for several blocks along Front Street. Metered parking is available on city streets. There are no covered facilities dockside, but several cafés and stores are located in the vicinity.

Island Ferry Adventures, which also operates a ferry to the Cape Lookout lighthouse from Harkers Island, runs

Nautical life is big in Morehead City.

regularly scheduled trips and guided tours to Shackleford and other islands. Its website offers thorough information about each destination and applicable ferry and tour services; hourly departures generally begin at 9 am seven days a week, in season.

Trips to Carrot Island take about 5 minutes; to the west end of Shackleford Banks, about 15 minutes.

618 Front St., Beaufort, NC 28516
Shackleford fare is $14 per adult round trip, 2 adult minimum. Reservations are not required but are highly recommended.
252.728.7555
www.islandferryadventures.com

On the Lookout Express you *will* get wet!

The **Lookout Express,** a 149-passenger speedboat with restrooms, covered seating area, and snack bar, is the largest ferry going to the Cape. The "big yellow boat" delivers masses of day-trippers to the Cape Lookout Lighthouse dock daily, traveling around on the ocean side due to its deeper draft. The firm also runs a Lighthouse Tour that takes travelers within close sight of—but not onto—the islands and operates excursion boats and dinner cruises.

410 Front St., Suite 2, Beaufort, NC 28516
Reservations by phone only; call for schedule
Half-day Lookout trip
$12 adults / $8 child / under 5 free
Half-day Early bird
$9 adults / $5 child / under 5 free
1.866.230.BOAT (1.866.230.2628)
252.728.6997, 252.728.7827
www.mysteryboattours.com

Outer Banks Ferry Service, located on the Beaufort waterfront across from the North Carolina Maritime Museum, is open

year-round and ferries passengers on 16-passenger skiffs to Cape Lookout, Carrot Island, and Shackleford Banks.

328 Front St., Beaufort, NC 28516
252.728.4129

Tour Beaufort

Marina Enterprises of Beaufort provides guided tours of Cape Lookout in summer, or a 15-minute ride to southern Shackleford Banks.

$22 adults / $15 children round trip
Call for schedule and reservations
252.342.0715

CAPE LOOKOUT NATIONAL SEASHORE AUTHORIZED FERRIES

Ferry services listed below are authorized by the National Park Service to provide transportation for visitors to the Cape Lookout National Seashore. Updated lists are posted periodically by the National Park Service on the Web at www.nps.gov/calo/ferry.htm and at the Visitor Center on Harkers Island. For additional information call 252.728.2250, 8.30 am–4.30 pm ET. After hours, a recording provides the list of ferry operators. Advance reservations are generally required.

passenger only
Morehead City to Shackleford Banks
    Waterfront Ferry Service   252.726.7678

passenger only
Beaufort to Shackleford Banks, Cape Lookout Lighthouse, South Core Banks
    Island Ferry Adventures   252.728.7555
    Mystery Tours   252.728.7827
    Outer Banks Ferry Service   252.728.4129

passenger only
Harkers Island to Shackleford Banks, Cape Lookout Lighthouse, South Core Banks
    Calico Jack's Ferry   252.728.3575
    Harkers Island Fishing Center   252.728.3907
    Island Ferry Adventures at Barbour's Marina   252.728.6181
    Local Yokel Ferry and Tours   252.728.2579

passenger or 4WD vehicle
Davis to South Core Banks, Great Island
    Great Island Cabins and Ferry Service   1.877.956.6568

passenger or 4WD vehicle
Atlantic to North Core Banks, Long Point
    Morris Marina Kabin Kamps and Ferry Service   252.225.4261

passenger only
Ocracoke to North Core Banks, Portsmouth Village
    Rudy Austin   252.928.4361

updated as of March 2007

Cape Lookout National Seashore / South Core Banks FERRY SCHEDULES

GETTING THERE

Map, pp. 122–23

Departs Harkers Island	Departs Cape Lookout
Seasonal or year-round schedules	
first departure 8.00 am	---
---	first return 8.30 am
Ferry schedules vary, but generally depart as early as 8 am and return as late as 5.30 pm, seven days a week, according to demand	
last departure 5.00 pm	
---	last return 5.30 pm

Morehead City, NC, to Harkers Island ferries
From downtown Morehead City, take US 70 E / Arendell St. east across the bridges to Beaufort, 4.1 miles. In downtown Beaufort, turn left (north) to stay on US 70. Follow US 70 E for 5.2 miles to the community of North River Center. (Look for East Carteret High School and the Cape Lookout sign.) Turn right (east) to stay on US 70 / Merrimon Rd., crossing the bridge over the North River and continuing 4.9 miles through the community of Bettie to the community of Otway. Turn right (south) onto Harkers Island Road / SR 1332 / SR 1335 (look for the large convenience store at the corner.) Proceed 5 miles through the community of Straits and across the drawbridge onto Harkers Island. As you bear left and continue on Harkers Island Rd., ferry landings will be on the right for the next four miles. The National Park Service Visitor Center is located at the end of Harkers Island Road.
Total est. distance: 20–23 miles
Total est. time: 40 minutes

Cedar Island, NC, to Harkers Island ferries
From the ferry landing at Cedar Island, take NC 12 for 12 miles west, past the Atlantic turnoff, to US 70 W. Proceed 16 miles, through the community of Davis (where you would turn off for the Great Island ferry) and turn left onto Harkers Island Road. Proceed 5 miles through the community of Straits and across the drawbridge onto Harkers Island. As you bear left and continue on Harkers Island Rd., ferry landings will be on the right for the next four miles. The National Park Service Visitor Center is located at the end of Harkers Island Road.
Total est. distance: 33–36 miles
Total est. time: 1 hour

Departs Davis mainland	Departs Cape Lookout
Seasonal or year-round schedules	
first departure 8.00 am	---
---	first return 8.30 am
Ferries generally make four runs daily	
last departure 5.00 pm	
---	last return 5.30 pm

Morehead City, NC, to ferry landing at Davis, NC
From downtown Morehead City, take US 70 E / Arendell St. east across the bridges to Beaufort, 4.1 miles. In downtown Beaufort, turn left (north) to stay on US 70. Follow US 70 E for 5.2 miles to the community of North River Center. (Look for East Carteret High School and the Cape Lookout sign.) Turn right (east) to stay on US 70 / Merrimon Rd., crossing the bridge over the North River and continuing 6.4 miles through the communities of Bettie and Otway to the stop sign in the community of Smyrna (where it's also possible to turn off for Harkers Island). Turn left to stay on US 70, following the ferry signs; proceed 6.1 miles to the community of Davis. At the stop sign turn right and then immediately left at the Great Island ferry sign.
Total est. distance: 22 miles
Total est. time: 40 minutes

passenger-only ferries

route Crosses Core Sound from town of **Harkers Island** (pop. 1,525, Carteret County) to Cape Lookout on **South Core Banks** (Carteret County)

duration 10–15 min

distance 4 to 8 mi

passenger/vehicle ferry

route Crosses Core Sound from town of **Davis** (pop. 442, Carteret County) to Long Point on **South Core Banks**

duration approx. 30 min

distance 5 to 6 mi

vessels, capacity, fare, schedule Vary according to destination, season, and day of week

reservations Required; call at least 24 hours ahead

terminal, shore facilities Harkers Island: passenger ferry landings, food, gas, and overnight accommodations; Davis: passenger/ vehicle ferry landings; restrooms, food, gas available during business hours

information A helpful, updated summary of authorized ferry services is found on the Cape Lookout Natitonal Seashore website at www.nps.gov/calo/ferry.htm

HARKERS ISLAND, HOME OF HARDY FISHING *and boatbuilding families, remains a world unto itself. Separated from the mainland by an old-fashioned drawbridge, its residents preserve bygone crafts and customs. Wooden boatbuilding, decoy carving, candlemaking, and storytelling testify to the self-sufficiency of the "Ca'e Bankers" (translated: Cape Bankers). Their brogue harks back to the Queen's English of earlier settlers.*

Leaving Beaufort on Highway 70, here a two-lane, narrow, curving road between soft shoulders and ditches, we can tell we're headed to a place like no other on the coast.

The Down East fishing boat is recognizable by its distinctive flared bow.

In mid-April, the woods and fields are full of purple cascades of wisteria, white dogwoods, pink shades of azaleas, trees greening up. Soon we begin to cross marsh creeks, reminding us how closely intermarried land and water are here.

Small craft are tied up behind a tree right next to the highway, in a way that reminds us of Louisiana bayous. A tall white egret stands in the ditch. We travel through the community of Bettie, where there are a few white-frame churches

and homes but not much else. Burying grounds for these small communities are located wherever there is a tiny plot of high ground, often right beside the road, fenced in for protection.

Across the drawbridge the welcome sign proclaims Harkers Island the "Gateway to Cape Lookout." The lighthouse is visible, far across the shallow sound, as clouds gather on the horizon and the breeze kicks up. As the locals have been known to say, "There's a lot of water in them sounds, but it's spread mighty thin."

ON HARKERS ISLAND CERTAIN family names recur: Pigott, Gaskill, Gillikin, Lewis. Road names in a couple of places mark the locations of former ferry landings, before the state ferry was moved to its current port on Cedar Island. The characteristic low-slung boat, with its sheltered bridge and flared bow, takes its name from this locale: the Core Sound fishing boat is a recognizable silhouette whether in the water, at the dock, or set up on dry land.

This remote island is home port for ferry and charter services that carry people and provisions over to the barrier islands. (For background on the Cape Lookout National Seashore, see the previous chapter.)

The Cape Lookout National Seashore Visitor Center and the National Park Service headquarters, at the east end of the road on Harkers Island, provide information on beach camping, driving, and safety. Ranger programs are also scheduled during warmer months, but you can learn a lot just within the walls of the center,

open every day but Christmas and New Year's Day. Recreational boating and kayak access are located near the visitor center; if you're headed over to the banks, you can file a float plan or register for camping here. There are public restrooms and a book and gift store on the premises, and a small picnic area across the road.

At the Core Sound Waterfowl Museum— now in its impressive new home next to the National Park Service center—decoy carvers and boatbuilders practice and teach their crafts. Each Down East community is represented by artifacts and documents that shed light on island life. Open year-round every day of the year except major holidays, the museum also provides a valuable resource for local history on its site, www.downeasttour. com. For more information on the museum: www.coresound.com, 252.728.1500.

Facilites and accommodations. On

Decoys and Down East culture await the visitor to the fascinating Core Sound Waterfowl Museum.

The Cape Lookout National Seashore Visitor Center is situated literally at the end of the road on Harkers Island.

Harkers Island there are several convenience stores with gas pumps, a small supermarket, three good restuarants at last count, a plethora of indepedent motels connected with the various marinas, an RV park, and even a couple of banks. One of the marinas also offers a spot for camping.

Signs for the ferry services are easy to spot along Harkers Island Road. All are on the right-hand side as you drive east.

•

The **Core Banks** take their name from the Coree Indians, who once left large oyster-shell middens in the region. Separated from the mainland by Core Sound, the banks are divided in two halves by Drum Inlet. On the far southern tip, near Beaufort Inlet and the Cape Lookout lighthouse, the natural harbor of the Bight is popular with recreational boaters. Nearby, the sheltered beach at the ferry landing is also an excellent spot for swimming and picnicing—all within sight of the majestic lighthouse.

The unmistakable diamond pattern of the Cape Lookout lighthouse dominates the horizon of the Core Banks.

The lighthouse was commissioned in 1804 and put into service in 1812. Some claim a mixup with the original paint schemes for this light and the one at Cape Hatteras (which protects Diamond Shoals) in the 1800s landed the Cape Lookout light with the diamond design intended for the other one. Whether the account is true or not, the Cape Lookout lighthouse remains a proud and distinctive icon of this part of the coast.

The lighthouse interior is closed to visitors except on limited occasions by advance reservation, but the island can be explored by boat, by foot, or by four-wheel-drive vehicle, and the former keeper's quarters has been put into use as a visitor center with interpretive exhibits and restrooms. Boardwalks

The calm waters of the Cape Lookout Bight invite swimmers on a hot summer's day.

provide easy access to the lighthouse and beaches. A new pavilion providing shade and restrooms was completed in summer 2006.

In years past, fishing camps sprang up all along the Core Banks on the sites of old whaling settlements. Even after the Park Service acquired lands for public use in the twentieth century, squatters constructed shacks and cabins, familiarly called "hooches". Today many of the camps remain popular fishing spots, and the **cabins** are available for rental to the public by reser-

vation. The Great Island cabins have very limited amenitites but accommodate 4 to 12 people. (More cabins are located at North Core Banks.) Primitive camping is allowed throughout the national seashore, at no cost, with some restrictions. Toilet facilities are extremely limited on the islands, and campers and visitors venturing away from the few improved areas must follow guidelines for proper disposal of human waste. All visitors must pack out whatever they've packed in.

Remoteness, solitude, and serenity are

exactly what most overnight visitors come for, though. (Well, that, and fish.) According to Cape Lookout ranger Karen Duggan, "They want that sense of quiet, dark skies, meteor showers . . . that's what they're looking for."

Duggan says that the National Park Service works diligently to help visitors have a good and safe experience. Rangers work with the licensed ferry operators, who are required to keep a log of visitors to the islands — and in case of severe weather, they work to make sure that everyone gets back to the mainland safely.

The ferries depart from varying locations along Island Road and customarily drop passengers off at the Lighthouse ferry dock at mile 41. If you want to transport a 4WD vehicle to South Core Banks (even for access to Cape Point), you'll depart from Davis, on the mainland, and arrive at the Great Island cabin area, near mile 28.

The lighthouse area offers day visitors the best amenities within the Cape Lookout National Seashore: a dock within easy walking distance of the lighthouse and visitor center, a pavilion for shade and restrooms, and a boardwalk over the dunes to the beach.

Cape Lookout from every angle: A nearby dock, a visitor center, a pavilion for shade, restrooms, and a boardwalk make for an easy visit to the lighthouse.

In Calico Jack's marina store: from left, Capt. Mike Cruise; Ethel Midgette; Capt. Rose Hatcher

HARKERS ISLAND

Calico Jack's Inn and Marina

Captain Mike Cruise looks forward to the end of the school year as eagerly as his science and P.E. students at Harkers Island Elementary do—because that's when he fills in as skipper on the ferry for Calico Jack's. This inn and marina complex, which has offered ferry service since 1990, includes a 22-room motel, a gift shop and tackle shop, and a small campground.

On an average summer day, they run three 16-passenger skiffs to the Cape, carrying 150 to 200 passengers, says Rose Hatcher, who with her husband, Donny, has owned and managed the operation for twelve years. "You meet a lot of nice people," she says. "It's a great business—you deal with a lot of tourists and families."

The ferry service runs seven days a week, weather permitting, 8.15 am–5 pm, from March through December; the trip takes about 8 to 10 minutes.

Calico Jack's also runs a 4WD-truck jitney service to carry passengers from the lighthouse area to the southern point of the cape. Reservations are required; the fee is $10 per passenger. Bookings may also be made via other Harkers Island ferry services.

Island Rd., PO Box 271,
Harkers Island, NC 28531
$10 adults / $6 children (extra fee for camping gear; vehicle parking fee also applies)
252.728.3575, 8 am–6 pm
www.capelookoutferry.com

Harkers Island Fishing Center

Rob Passfield has owned and operated this motel and marina for the past fourteen years. He runs a daily ferry to Cape Lookout, South Core Banks, and Shackleford Banks from 8.45 am to 5 pm, between Easter and Thanksgiving. The crossing takes about 10 to

15 minutes depending on the tide, and he's happy to drop passengers wherever they want to go.

1002 Island Rd., PO Box 400,
Harkers Island, NC 28531
Two 16-passenger vessels
$10 adults / $6 children 12 and under, round trip
Parking on site is free for day visitors, $3/night for overnight visitors
Call ahead 24 hours for group reservation
252.728.3907
www.harkersmarina.com
info@harkersmarina.com

Island Ferry Adventures

Captain Bo Anderson, Captain Chuck Marriner, and Captain Caroline Corwin ferry passengers to the Banks in Island Ferry's 16-passenger skiffs. The ferry departs from Barbour's Marina on demand or by reservation. Parking is available on-site; the marina, under new ownership in 2006, offers a comfortable ship's store with a deck overlooking the sound.

Barbour's Harbor Marina
1390 Island Rd., Harkers Island, NC 28531
252.728.6181
www.barboursmarina.com

The Local Yokel

The first ferry service visitors encounter after crossing to the island, Ellis Yeomans's Local Yokel is located on the right. Parking is free on-site; there is a small gift store. Departures begin at 8 am (earlier departures available); it's a 5-minute trip to Shackleford Banks and 12 minutes to Cape Lookout.

516 Island Rd., Harkers Island, NC 28531
$10 adults / $6 children
252.728.2759

Captain Caroline makes the run to Cape Lookout look easy in Island Ferry Adventures' 24' Carolina Skiff.

The crew of the Local Yokel assist passengers off at the Harkers Island dock.

DAVIS

The hamlet of **Davis** has one convenience store and five churches. There is gas available in Davis—but you'd probably do better to stock up on groceries for your OBX trip back in Morehead City. Davis offers no mainland lodging or dining (there's a café up the road in Atlantic).

Off US 70 N, turn right at the Texaco station, following the sign to Core Banks. Alger Willis Fishing Camps ran the Davis concession for several years but has recently been replaced by Morris Marina's services. (To reach the Cedar Island ferry, turn left at this same intersection.) If you're traveling these roads in inclement weather or after dark, be especially careful, as the shoulder slopes dramatically into the canal or marsh.

Getting to Great Island

The passenger and four-wheel-drive vehicle ferry service to South Core Banks is a third-generation operation, explains Annette Willis Mitchum, who staffs the ferry office in Davis

Pay close attention: from Davis, N.C., roads lead to three different ferry terminals!

these days. Back in the 1950s, her grandparents, Alger Willis, Sr., and Jeannette, ran a boardinghouse on the mainland and carried visitors over to the Banks, primarily for recreational fishing. The guests built cabins—little more than shacks—and eventually the Willises improved them and rented them out.

"We've had some visitors coming for forty years or more," Mitchum says with pride. "Now they're bringing their children and grandchildren."

Unlike the popular lighthouse area eleven miles south, which attracts a fair number of day visitors and backpackers, the Great Island cabin area primarily draws visitors with vehicles who intend to stay overnight in the cabins. The cabins tend to be a bit more on the rustic side than their counterparts on North Core Banks (they lack electricity), but all have hot water and bathrooms, and there is a caretaker on site. Shower and bathroom facilities are provided for day visitors and campers.

Following a recent change in management, Morris Marina and Kabin Kamps of Atlantic, N.C., leases two vessels from Alger Willis Fishing Camps and manages the ferries and the cabin concession.

The ferry operates mid-March through early December. The *Captain Alger* carries 4 vehicles and 49 passengers; the smaller *Kathryn T.* handles 2 vehicles and 28 passengers. Reservations for holidays and the busy fall fishing season book up months in advance; in summer, a few days' notice is usually required.

Great Island Cabin and Ferry Service

142 Willis Road, Davis, NC 28524
Reservations via Morris Marina and Kabin Camps:
1.877.9.LOOKOUT / 1.877.956.6568
252.225.4261
www.capelookoutconcessions.com

Two vessels operating from Davis carry visitors and properly equipped vehicles to the South Core Banks.

Cape Lookout National Seashore / North Core Banks FERRY SCHEDULE

Departs Atlantic mainland	Departs Long Point
Seasonal schedule March–December	
7.00 am	---
---	8.00 am
9.00 am	---
	10.00 am
11.00 am	---
---	12.00 noon
3.00 pm	---
---	4.00 pm

GETTING THERE

Map, pp. 122–23

Morehead City, NC, to Atlantic, NC
From downtown Morehead City, take US 70 E / Arendell St. east across the bridges to Beaufort, 4.1 miles. In downtown Beaufort, turn left (north) at Live Oak St. to stay on US 70. Follow US 70 E for 5.2 miles to the community of North River Center. (Look for East Carteret High School and the Cape Lookout sign.) Turn right (east) to stay on US 70 / Merrimon Rd., crossing the bridge over the North River and continuing 6.4 miles through the communities of Bettie and Otway to the stop sign in the community of Smyrna (where it's also possible to turn off for Harkers Island). Turn left to stay on US 70, following the ferry signs; proceed 6.1 miles to the community of Davis. Turn left to stay on US 70; proceed 8.2 miles to the intersection with NC 12 (the turnoff for the Cedar Island Ferry). Bear right on US 70 toward Sea Level and proceed 4.5 miles to the eastern terminus of US 70 in Atlantic. Turn left one block and then right on Morris Marina Rd. Proceed 0.7 miles to the ferry terminal, at the end of the road.
Total est. distance: 35.2 miles
Total est. time: 1 hour

Cedar Island, NC, to Atlantic ferry landing
From the ferry landing at Cedar Island, take NC 12 for 10 miles west. Turn left (southeast) at Old Cedar Island Rd. Proceed 3.1 miles to Morris Marina Rd. Turn left and proceed 0.7 miles to the ferry terminal, at the end of the road.
Total est. distance: 12 miles
Total est. time: 20 minutes

CAPE LOOKOUT NATIONAL SEASHORE
← SOUTH CORE BANKS
VIA TOLL FERRY

CHAPTER 13

Cape Lookout National Seashore North Core Banks

passenger/4WD vehicle ferry

route Crosses central Core Sound from town of **Atlantic** (pop. 1,744, Carteret County) to **Cape Lookout National Seashore, Long Point, North Core Banks** (Carteret County)

duration 45–60 min to Long Point

distance 2 mi

vessels/capacity *Donza Lee,* 8 vehicles, 49 pasengers; *Green Grass,* 4 vehicles, 49 passengers

fare Adult passenger, round trip, $14; vehicle, one way, $17.50–$65 and up; additional fees for extra gear or guided Portsmouth trip

schedule Departures at 7, 9, and 11 am and 3 pm; returns at 8 and 10 am, 12 noon, and 4 pm daily March–December

terminal 1000 Morris Marina Rd., Atlantic, NC 28511

reservations Call ahead, 252.225.4261

information www.portsmouthislandfishing.com

shore facilities Restaurant, restrooms, telephone, parking

fact The *Donza Lee* is the largest private ferry in the state.

ATLANTIC'S SLOGAN IS "LIVING FROM THE SEA," *and people here have just about no other choice. They work in fisheries, seafood packing and sales, boatbuilding, engine repair, or the ferry business. Not much happens here if it doesn't involve water.*

Shell Road leads from the village out to the Morris Marina, a combination port, repair facility, and neighborhood bar. It's late afternoon by now, and the sun has managed to peek weakly out from behind clouds.

The Morris Grill features a deck over the water—pleasant enough on a sunny day, but too exposed for this raw, windy spring afternoon. Only a black setter, lounging under a plastic chair, endures the chill.

Inside, patrons can take their choice of a solitary video poker machine, a friendly game of eight-ball at the pool table, or counter service. Camo, it's clear, is the accepted dress, domestic draft the preferred beverage. I'm ready for a bit of a sugar fix but don't have time to linger if I'm going to make the four o'clock Cedar Island ferry to Ocracoke.

"Anything for dessert?" I ask the waitress.

"Budweiser," replies one smart-aleck customer, before she can answer.

Morris Marina Bar & Grill, Atlantic

The clock on the wall reads "Time for Fishing." The lamp over the pool table is embellished with a backwards-slanting "8." It's sportsmen's territory for sure, and if the fish aren't biting or it's between game seasons, there's still likely to be a lively pre-race chat.

"How about coffee, then?"

"Just turned the pot off. But I could brew you some."

"Maybe just a Coke," I suggest. Forget the Diet. If only I had time to stick around for the legendary shrimp burger . . . but that'll have to wait till the next trip this way.

MORRIS MARINA IS CAPE CANAVERAL for missions to **North Core Banks**—all expeditions launch from here. On a busy day in summer or in high fishing season, the loading and unloading of vehicles and gear is a demanding business.

Ann Noyes is on duty in Mission Control—the small office toward the end of the parking lot. That's where you'll claim your cabin and ferry reservation and pay your toll. She dispatches phone calls with cool efficiency and fields questions from folks waiting in line for the 9 am boat—which is half an hour late returning this morning.

The crew of the *Donza Lee* return from Long Point with a full load.

Loading up for the Banks requires backing onto the boat.

A radio communication from the bridge of the *Donza Lee,* inbound with a fully loaded vessel, solves the mystery: a truck pulling a Scout trailer had gotten stuck in the sand and had to be completely unpacked before it could be pulled out, driven onto the ferry, and repacked. And as it happened on this ninety-degree day, it was the vehicle first in line.

Getting vehicles out of fixes, loading the large ferry safely, and navigating knee-deep waters are only some of the challenges Captain Josh Arthur faces every working day. But he deals with them like a pro, getting the boat back to port and waving a gracious good-bye to the Boy Scouts before turning around to load up again.

The boat he skippers today was designed by the late Don Morris, who with his father, Ira Morris, founded the ferry operation here in the 1940s and for whom the boat

is named. After Don Morris passed away in 1996, the vessel was completed in 1998 and commissioned the follwing year by his widow. When Katie Morris also passed away, her daughter, Kari Martin, took over the business and still runs it today; Kari's brother Mark manages the Great Island ferry at Davis.

At a time when employment in the marine and nautical industries is suffering Down East, Captain Josh is glad to have a place in this family-owned business. He just might wish folks would learn to let a *little* more air out of their tires.

•

Driving on the Banks, as folks who have done it will tell you, isn't like Daytona. To prepare for deep, soft sand or flooded stretches, you'll almost certainly need four-wheel drive. The National Park Service distributes helpful information on items (like boards and sand shovel) to take with you in the event you do get stuck; don't ignore their good advice, and

Shallow water is a constant challenge for boats in Core Sound.

Vehicles bound for the beach are rigged for maximum off-road efficiency.

that a motorized vehicle is essential to haul enough gear and supplies for a week-long or weekend fishing trip. Coolers are needed for perishables and your catch; there are no refrigerators in the Long Point cabins. There is electricity, provided by a large solar bank and backed up by generators. Although the cabins are furnished, you'll need to take all cookware, utensils, and bedding. Add to that your fishing equipment and a few clothes appropriate to the weather, and you've got more than most folks are willing to pack in on foot. And if you want to go up to the northern end of the island and visit Portsmouth Village, you'll definitely need transportation to get there.

The cabins are located within sight of the ferry dock. There is a caretaker onsite, and if extra provisions are needed, an order can be sent back via the next ferry. For those who enjoy roughing it, tent camping is permitted anywhere on the seashore, subject to a few restrictions. Whichever way you go, on North Core Banks you're definitely "away from it all."

•

do decrease the air pressure in all tires (including those on any trailer you're towing). The marina has an air hose for refilling tires upon your return.

Before you decide to venture over with the brand-new all-wheel-drive Escalade, you might also take a look at some of the photos on various Outer Banks websites. The effects of tide and weather can be unpredictable. As one park ranger put it, "Don't drive anything out there that you couldn't afford to give up as an expensive gift to the sea."

Most visitors to North Core Banks find

"Welcome to Stacy, pop. 205."

On US 70 between Davis and **Atlantic** you drive past wide, flat stretches of water on one side—and wide, flat stretches of land on the other. Dry land extends narrow fingers out into the water, which encroaches from every angle around each new bend. Stiles are laid across the ditches, to provide access to houses and boathouses. Newer homes are built on piers, but many older ones look as though they would simply float away if the water were to rise another inch.

Some 44,000 acres of fields here in

Carteret County comprise the Open Ground Farm, one of the largest agricultural operations east of the Mississippi. A great deal of fenced acreage also constitutes the Marine Corps Outlying Landing Field—a topic of controversy between defense and industry interests and environmental advocates who claim the huge, noise-creating installation disturbs migratory birds and alters the composition of wetlands.

Nature reaches in close here. Blackbirds rest in the branches of wax myrtles by the roadside. Herons and egrets wade in the canals and ditches. Cormorants, their black necks snaking forward, plow and dive in the shallow creeks. Birds and fish are still infinitely more plentiful than people, and most Down East residents and visitors like it that way.

Likewise, short-term **overnight accommodations** for visitors are sparse. You won't find a chain motel closer than Morehead City. The Driftwood Motel at the end of Cedar Island is a comfortable choice. For a more luxurious stay, the Otway House Bed & Breakfast, which opened in 2004, is twenty miles back west on US 70. The Sea Level Inn has been converted to retirement condominiums after a long stint as the motel and restaurant (now discontinued) serving the original Ocracoke ferry, which once operated from this soundside hamlet.

Otherwise, eastern Carteret County offers only a few private campgrounds for tents or RVs. A particular favorite is the Cedar Creek Campground on Styron Bay outside Sea Level, a secret we're recultantly sharing here.

In Atlantic, you'll find the the Red & White Supermarket, the Cruise Mart (hardware, marine supplies, and gas) and the post office. Handy House convenience stores with Texaco gas are located back at the intersections in Davis and Smyrna—but neither is open round the clock. In Otway, at the turnoff to Harkers Island, there is a 24-hour convenience store with gas and food.

Restaurants are equally infrequent— again, the Driftwood and the Morris Marina Grill are about it. Sea Level, with its renowned Snug Harbor retirement community, has medical and hospital facilities available. (Snug Harbor, founded in New York in 1801 as a rest home for those retired from the merchant marine, moved to the more hospitable Carolina coast In 1976.)

Morris Marina Kabin Kamps and Ferry Service

Departures from Atlantic at 7 am, 9 am, 11 am, and 3 pm daily, March—mid-December Returns from Long Point at 8 am, 10 am, 12 noon, and 4 pm daily

1000 Morris Marina Rd., Atlantic, NC 28511
Fares $14 per passenger (children under 6 free), $35 per ATV, $75–$130 per vehicle; additional fee applies for extra gear
1.877.9.LOOKOUT / 1.877.956.6568
252.225.4261
www.capelookoutconcessions.com

Cape Lookout National Seashore / Portsmouth Island FERRY SCHEDULE

GETTING THERE

Map, pp. 122–23

To ferry landing at Ocracoke Village, NC
Travel to Ocracoke village by way of ferry or taking NC 12 south on Ocracoke Island. The ferry dock is located on Silver Lake Road, behind the grocery store in on Silver Lake harbor.

Departs Ocracoke	Departs Portsmouth Village
Seasonal or year-round schedules	
first departure 8.00 am	---
---	first return 8.30 am
Ferry schedules depart as early as 8 am and return as late as 5.30 pm, seven days a week, according to demand	
last departure 5.00 pm	
---	last return 5.30 pm

By 1956, a postage stamp was the only item that could still be purchased on once-thriving Posrtmouth Island. The post office closed in 1959, though a handful of residents remained until the 1970s.

CHAPTER 14

Cape Lookout National Seashore Portsmouth Village

passenger-only ferry
See previous chapter for information on reaching Portsmouth Island via Atlantic, NC, or transporting vehicles

route Crosses Ocracoke Inlet from village of **Ocracoke** (pop. 750, Hyde County) to village of **Portsmouth** (uninhabited), on North Core Banks (Carteret County)

duration 20 min

distance 4 mi

vessels and capacity 24′ skiff; 16 passengers

fare $20

reservations
Call ahead, 24 hours in advance

schedule
8 am–5.30 pm daily, on demand

terminal and information
Dock adjacent to Annabelle's Florist in Ocracoke Village 252.928.4361 / 252.928.5431 Web www.austinboattours.com

shore facilities In Ocracoke, dock with access to restrooms; convenience store nearby. In Portsmouth Village, limited restroom facilities near ferry dock; Visitor Center open intermittently in season

RUDY AUSTIN'S WIFE ANSWERS THE PHONE, *and I apologize for interrupting their dinner when I call to double-check if the boat's going to run tomorrow. He assures me it will. And no problem about the call, he says—better to make certain about preparations.*

Captain Rudy has made a career of shuttling riders back and forth between his hometown of Ocracoke and the surrounding

Portsmouth: a ferry trip back in time

islands, and these days, now that he and his brother have taken over the passenger ferry business started by their late father, he makes several 20-minute crossings daily (scheduled or as needed) to the dock at deserted Portsmouth Village.

On Saturday morning a gaggle of backpack-toting tourists gather on Capt. Rudy's dock, eager for an expedition to Ports-

IT IS CUSTOMARY
TO TIP YOUR

Rudy Austin (left) continues the ferry service begun by his father.

mouth Island. Ten of us—kids of all ages—accompany him in the 24' skiff. (The Austins used to use a larger excursion boat, but shoaling in the channel after recent hurricanes has forced them to rely on the smaller flat-bottomed craft). The boat zips past the pelican rookery on Beacon Island and a lone hunting cabin on a tiny marsh island all to itself, and rounds the point where the village comes in view.

We note our pickup time and site, hoist our cameras and water bottles, and take turns dousing each other with bug spray. Visitors returning from the village yesterday have advised that the flies and mosquitoes have begun to make their appearance for the season. That turns out to be a monumental understatement.

Even on a cool and breezy May morning,

the insects are too active to allow a leisurely exploration of the buildings, which are surrounded by the luxuriant swaths of the green grasses and thickets bugs so love. No one sticks around long. We fairly sprint to the tide flats and the beaches, where we hope to find some relief from the swarms.

On the island, the only amenities (that word is used loosely) are a few composting toilets far from the beach, a single source of potable water, and the scant rest stop offered by a couple of rocking chairs on the porch of the main house. That's it. No phone, no food or drink concessions, and—most important to note—no shade or seating once you've walked a mile to the beach.

But isolation is the thing so many of us come to seek, and Portsmouth rewards us amply. The *only crowds here are the fish and the gulls. It's a paradise of seashells, from impressive-sized welks to countless scallops to rare scotch bonnets.*

On the beach, which is wide and flat, a trio of ATVs roll past us. (Capt. Rudy's son runs the Portsmouth ATV Excursions out of Ocracoke, providing island access to those who aren't mobile enough to hike.) A guy out on the point is pulling in all the puppy drum he can manage, while his kids frolic in the tidal pools. (Good thing he's in a truck; a few 4WD vehicles venture up here after crossing on the car ferry from Atlantic.)

Everyone spreads out towels for picnic lunches. Afterwards some of us nap, some wade, some walk. When it's time to go, Captain Rudy meets us at the designated spot. He eases the skiff expertly into a cove, waits for us to slide in over the bow, then poles us out of knee-deep water until he can safely gun the engine again. He's as

knowledgeable a tour guide as skipper, regaling us with accounts of everything from Blackbeard's exploits to legendary storms, from the habits of shorebirds to real estate development on the Outer Banks. As we tie up at the dock and step off the boat, we all agree on one thing: it's been a terrific experience, and we'd do it again. But maybe in November when the bugs are gone.

MOST VISITORS to **Portsmouth** arrive, like us, at the Haulover dock on the marsh side of the island. The village, the only ghost town on the eastern seaboard, is located here at the northern end by the inlet, where during the era of sail the oceangoing ships would offload their cargoes onto lighter craft to be carried across to the mainland.

Up until the early twentieth century Portsmouth did a brisk trade, supporting its own schools, church, post office, stores, and U.S. Life-Saving Station. But the shipping business eventually moved elsewhere, and the last determined residents gave up their solitude and moved inland in 1971. The cluster of cottages and buildings remain nearly

In 1770 Portsmouth was the largest settlement on the Outer Banks; today, it is uninhabited.

PORTSMOUTH

Capt. Rudy Austin
Daily trips from Ocracoke
PO Box 375, Ocracoke NC 27960
252.928.4361

Capt. Donald Austin
PO Box 375, Ocracoke NC 27960
252.928.5431

Portsmouth Island ATV Excursions
All-terrain vehicle tours are run by Rudy
Austin's son. One person per ATV; drivers
must be at least 16, with valid driver's license. They provide the ATVs and do not take
personal ATVs. They also have a Kawasaki
Mule to provide access to passengers who
would not otherwise get to experience the
island.

Two tours daily, 8 am–noon and 1–5 pm,
weather permitting
252.928.4484
www.portsmouthislandatvs.com

intact as an artifact of their times, although
Hurricane Isabel did extensive damage here
in 2003. No one lives in the village—or
elsewhere on the island—except a couple of
intrepid Park Service volunteers who do six-
week stints in the mild seasons as caretakers.

There is a visitor center on site, staffed
by volunteers. There are restroom facilities in
the village. But you'll need to bring your own
water, food, and insect repellent. Correction:
you'll need to bring *lots* of insect repellent.

To get more of the flavor of the place,
read the novel *Sea-Born Women* (2002) by
B. J. Mountford, who once spent a season
here as a park volunteer.

Facilities on Portsmouth Island, such as these
composting toilets, are minimal.

Below: Graves of the Grace family, Portsmouth Village. Right: Baptist and Methodist churches once formed a hub of village life; today, the Methodist church still stands, rebuilt following a 1913 fire.

Elwell Ferry, Cape Fear River, Bladen County

the **last** of the state's **river ferries**

HOLDOVERS FROM THE ERA OF FLAT-BOTTOMED WOODEN FERRIES secured by rope and maneuvered by pole, the cable-guided river ferries still carry motor vehicles—two at a time—across remote stretches of North Carolina's waterways. The remaining three river ferries in the state have been managed by the North Carolina Department of Transportation since 1931, when the government took over highways and ferries.

The "home base" of each ferry is on the northern bank of the river. So if you approach from the south and don't happen to catch the ferry operator finishing up a run, you must blow your car horn to signal the operator to bring the boat over to your side. Don't let the wait stop you. The short ride is free, it's scenic, and it's a rare glimpse at an earlier time.

Sans Souci Ferry, Cashie River, Bertie County

Elwell Ferry
SCHEDULE

Map and directions, pp. 170–71

	Carvers to Kelly
	Year-round schedule
first crossing 6.00 am*	---
Ferry runs on demand throughout the day, seven days a week	
---	last crossing 6.00 pm*
* Ferry may operate dawn to dusk during winter months	

Elwell Ferry
Cape Fear River

cable-guided vehicle ferry

route Connects NC Hwy. 53 (east bank) with NC Hwy. 87 (west bank); crosses Cape Fear River from town of **Kelly** (pop. 454, Bladen County) to community of **Carvers** (Bladen County)

duration 5 min

distance 150 yards

vessels One cable ferry (capacity 2 cars, 17 passengers)

fare Free

reservations No

schedule 6.00 am–6.00 pm daily on demand, year-round

information www.kellync.org

shore facilities West/southern bank: Public boat launching ramp; East/northern bank: small covered picnic shelter and tables with grill. No pay phone, vending machines, or other facilities nearby on either shore.

THEY GATHER AT THE RIVER, FOUR GENERATIONS *of Russ kinfolk and friends. "Right there—that's where I swam across the Cape Fear River as a kid," recalls one of the women, pointing to a place slightly downstream from the landing. "And back then the bank was so grown up, when I got to the other side the current had carried me farther downstream than I intended, and there was no place to climb up—I had to turn right around and swim back!"*

The current is stronger here than it looks, and the water is deep, probably twenty feet or more where the river curves and narrows

Descendants of ferrymen Walter and John Russ, October 2005

at the ferry. For a hundred years, the Russes and others in the Kelly community of rural Bladen County have operated this crossing. On October 15, 2005, their descendants have come together

The old Kelly Baptist Church, near the Elwell Ferry, is now the Kelly Museum

with friends and community to celebrate the ferry's hundredth birthday—complete with eulogies for the founders, singing of "The Star-Spangled Banner," and birthday cake in the hall of the former Baptist church that is now the community's historical museum.

The church pews are full, every folding chair occupied. The old upright piano does the patriotic tunes proud. At the rear of the former baptistry, the mural of the River Jordan resembles another river, closer by. The stair rail angles down in a way that could almost be taken for the cable that holds the ferryboat steady against the current.

The celebration is part revival and dinner on the grounds, part family reunion. Kelly Historical Society president Richard Smith calls

all of the "ferry family" to the front and introduces them. The meeting closes with "America the Beautiful" and hugs and greetings. The guests will have the rest of a golden autumn afternoon to share memories and pictures.

And how could they end their special day, but to drive a couple miles down to the Cape Fear and board the current-day ferryboat for a ride? The Spanish moss hangs low over the water, the greens and golds reflect on the smooth surface of the river, the boat floats silently at the bank. Its ramp waits, open, like the arms of an old friend.

TO GET TO THE ELWELL FERRY from Burgaw in neighboring Pender County, you really have to know where you're going — you won't come upon it by accident. (As the town's website proclaims, "Some maps don't show Kelly, some do. It's a secret that we're willing to share with you.") Burgaw, the small-town county seat, is as good a starting place as any, but a maze of interweaving country highways and back roads can lull you into watching the pastures and forests and not the road signs.

Two-lane NC Highway 53 passes through the hamlet of **Atkinson** and crosses over the Black River. There NC 11 will split off, headed toward Freeman. Just stay on NC 53 toward White Lake. You'll cross NC 210, which goes to Moores Creek National Battlefield (worth a side trip if you have time).

Soon you come to the **Kelly** community, which amounts to a clutch of churches, a historical marker, a fire department, a florist shop, and a post office. There's one part-time gas station with two pumps and a pay phone. (If you're coming this way late or early, be sure to get gas no later than Ward's Corner, the station at the intersection with US 421; if you're coming from the other side of the river, get gas in Tar Heel or Elizabethtown. And watch out for logging trucks and other large vehicles on these curving roads.)

The Elwell Ferry has been transporting people and their vehicles—two cars at a time—for more than a century. (Photo from Elwell Ferry historical website)

Two miles past Kelly, look for the Trinity United Methodist Church and a small sign indicating Elwell Ferry Road, on the left. The paved road ends at a well-maintained landing complete with picnic shelter and grill. (I'd bring bug spray if I were coming here to sit for any length of time—the mosquitoes, flies, dragonflies, and no-see-ums are powerfully active.) The swamp comes right up to the edges of the shaded lane, so it's easy to see that this way can flood in heavy rain.

To the right of the loading ramp is a

white wooden tower housing the cable stays and the winch that's used to lower the cable at night.

In the mid-1800s, when Joseph Elwell owned the land hereabouts and lent his name to the spot as Elwell Landing, steamboats plied the Cape Fear carrying goods and passengers upstream to Fayetteville or downstream to Wilmington. The boats called at "flag stops," rural landings where a flag or campfire was used to signal a request to board riders or cargo.

According to J. R. McKoy and C. A. Carter in their centennial edition of the ferry's history, Elwell Landing was a popular gathering spot for socializing as well. Its tranquility, natural beauty, and down-home friendliness are little changed today. Although steamboat traffic began to decline after the turn of the twentieth century, a way was soon needed to transport wagons (and eventually automobiles) across the river, and Elwell looked like a promising site for a ferry.

Entrepreneurial brothers Walter and John Russ petitioned for the county contract to establish the ferry, and construction of the first wooden flatboat and grading of roads to the landings soon began.

At first the boat was poled upstream and rowed back by hand. The 33-foot ferryboat could carry a wagon and two mules. The county subsidized its operation six days a week so that the public traveled for free, but if Walter Russ had to run the ferry on a Sunday, the toll was a quarter—fifty cents after dark.

Walter Russ raised his sons to operate the ferry from an early age. Under the expert guidance of the Russes, the ferry carried cotton to the gin, crops to market, doctors to house calls, pastors to their congregations, children to school. During the years of Prohibition, it almost certainly also carried well-hidden cargoes of locally distilled illegal liquor.

Delightful tales of minor mishaps in the ferry's early era abound. In the days when cars were still newfangled contraptions for farmers used to horses and mules, several vehicles suffered dunking in the river, though no lives were lost.

Walter Russ himself, sadly, became the ferry's first fatality. In the 1930s the state of North Carolina began to take over the ferries as part of the state highway system. The state installed the first cable and provided larger boats that could be guided along it with a pull stick. Russ, still employed on the route he had initiated years earlier, saw the ferry through this stage of modernization as well as the addition, in the late 1930s, of a gasoline-powered engine on the boat.

Russ, who had warned that inadequate ventilation of the engine might prove hazardous, was killed in a March 1942 explosion caused by that very condition. A year after the tragic accident the ferry was rebuilt and reinstated with safety improvements. It has been operated since then by a succession of ferrymen (including Walter's son Lee Roy). Its wooden construction has been replaced by steel and its gas engine by diesel.

These days, bridges over the Cape Fear carry much more car and truck traffic than the ferry. Better highways make a few extra miles easily tolerable for most travelers. But, as one of the ferrykeepers here told me quite sincerely one day, "It'll save you quite a bit of time, depending on where you're going."

•

Bladen County, called North Carolina's "Mother County" because so many others were carved out of its original configuration, is defined by its topography and natural history. The Black, South, and Cape Fear Rivers drain the region, which is marked by numerous streams, shallow lakes, and mysterious Carolina bays. Fishing and boating are popular pastimes on these waters.

White Lake (14 miles from the Elwell Ferry) is the largest of the white-sand-bottom pocosin lakes. It was developed into a recreational resort as far back as 1901, and the vintage motels and cottages that sit shoulder-to-shoulder around the lake's perimeter impart a funky 1950s flavor to the community. The lake is billed as "the nation's safest beach" for swimming, and an amusement park and a nearby 18-hole golf course provide other recreational opportunities.

There is a large RV camground at the entrance to White Lake; camping is also available at **Jones Lake State Park** (4 miles outside Elizabethtown on NC 242), which features newly upgraded swimming, bathhouse, picnic, and visitor center facilities. Though Singletary Lake State Park is located near the ferry, on NC 53, camping is limited to registered nonprofit groups.

A short ways south of the ferry on NC 87 is the Lock and Dam #1 on the Cape Fear River, one of several that make the waterway navigable for small craft. The lock is an excellent, isolated spot for fishing, camping, and picnicking. A public picnic shelter and a private campground are located at the end of the road.

The only other hostelry in the county is a Days Inn in **Elizabethtown,** the county seat, 26 miles from the ferry. Lodgings can be found farther afield in Whiteville and Wilmington on the southern/eastern side or Wallace, in Duplin County, on the northern/western side.

On Broad Street in Elizabethtown, you'll fare a bit better for homestyle dining, with casual eateries and sandwich shops. Melvin's, once the lunch of choice, has gone out of business, but hey, there's a McDonald's.

Burgaw, though it's still a goodly drive from the ferry, has the advantage of proximity to I-40, so there are several cafes and fast-food restaurants. For nostalgia's sake, order lunch at the counter in Dee's Drugstore on the square, or drive down to Paul's Famous Hot Dogs in **Rocky Point.**

To best understand the history and people of this neck of the woods, read Carolyn Rawls Booth's novels *Between the Rivers* (2001) and its sequel *Bandeaux Creek* (2005). For a detailed account of the Elwell Ferry's history, read *Elwell Ferry, Kelly, North Carolina* (2005), edited by J.

R. McKoy and C. A. Carter with afterwords by Vera Heath Russ and Sylvia Kay Russ Andress.

For more information
- Elizabethtown–White Lake Chamber of Commerce, www.elizabethtownwhitelake.com, 910.862.4368
- Burgaw Area Chamber of Commerce, www.burgawchamber.com, 910.259.9817
- Pender County Tourism, in the historic Burgaw Train Depot, www.visitpender.com, 1.888.576.4756

Burgaw's Blueberry Festival celebrates agriculture—and summer fun.

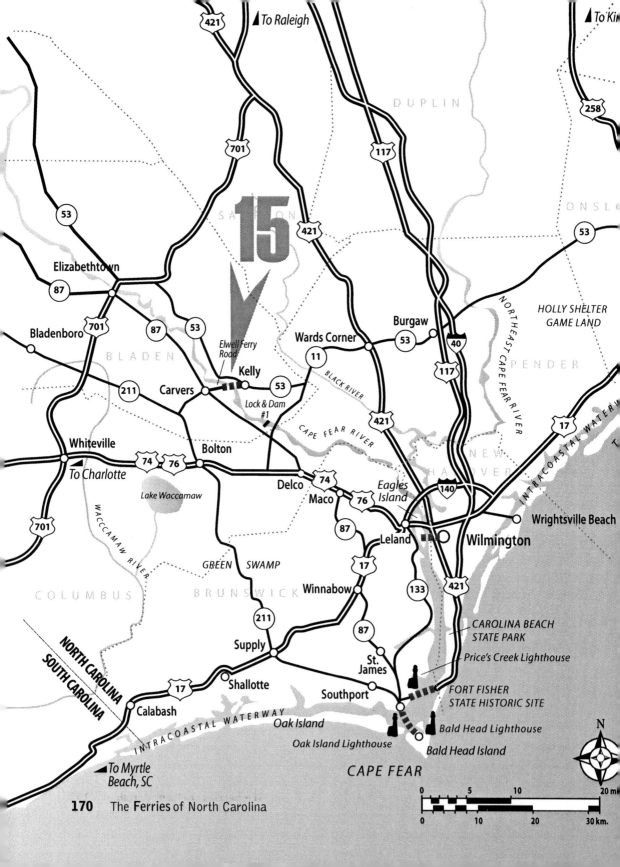

To Raleigh

421

To Ki

258

DUPLIN

701

117

53

ONSL

15

Elizabethtown

87

53

701

Bladenboro

87

53

Elwell Ferry Road

Wards Corner

Burgaw

53

HOLLY SHELTER GAME LAND

BLADEN

Kelly

11

40

211

Carvers

53

117

Lock & Dam #1

BLACK RIVER

421

Whiteville

74   76

To Charlotte

701

Bolton

CAPE FEAR RIVER

Delco

74

Maco

Eagles Island

NEW

140

NORTHEAST CAPE FEAR RIVER

PENDER

17

Lake Waccamaw

76

HANOVER

INTRACOASTAL WATERWAY

T

87

Leland

Wilmington

Wrightsville Beach

WACCAMAW RIVER

GREEN   SWAMP

17

Winnabow

133

COLUMBUS

BRUNSWICK

211

87

421

CAROLINA BEACH STATE PARK

NORTH CAROLINA
SOUTH CAROLINA

Supply

St. James

Price's Creek Lighthouse

17

Shallotte

Southport

FORT FISHER STATE HISTORIC SITE

Calabash

Oak Island

Oak Island Lighthouse

Bald Head Lighthouse

Bald Head Island

To Myrtle Beach, SC

INTRACOASTAL WATERWAY

CAPE FEAR

N

0   5   10   20 mi

0   10   20   30 km.

170   The **Ferries** of North Carolina

Elwell Ferry   GETTING THERE

Wilmington, NC, to Elwell Ferry landing (south/west side of Cape Fear River)

From downtown Wilmington cross the Cape Fear Memorial Bridge; take US 74/76 west 17 miles to intersection with NC 87 N. Turn right (north) toward Elizabethtown; proceed 16 miles past the International Paper Plant at Riegelwood, past the turnoff to the lock/dam on the Cape Fear River, to the community of Carvers. (Look for Oakland Plantation / Johnson Turf Farms and the historic site of Ashwood Plantation, seat of the Bartram family.) Turn right (northeast) on SR 1730 / N. Elwell Ferry Road. Proceed 2.6 miles to the ferry landing.
Total est. distance: 35.6 miles
Total est. time: 50 minutes

Elizabethtown, NC, to Elwell Ferry landing (south/west side of Cape Fear River)

From downtown Elizabethtown take NC 87 / E Broad St. 16.3 miles southeast to the community of Carvers. (Look for Oakland Plantation / Johnson Turf Farms and the historic site of Ashwood Plantation, seat of the Bartram family.) Turn left (northeast) on SR 1730 / N. Elwell Ferry Road. Proceed 2.6 miles to the ferry landing.
Total est. distance: 19 miles
Total est. time: 50 minutes

Burgaw, NC, to Elwell Ferry landing (north/east side of Cape Fear River)

From downtown Burgaw take NC 53 west through to communities of Wards Corner, Atkinson, and Long View 26 miles to the community of Kelly. Proceed 2 miles further on NC 53 and turn left (south) on SR 1730 / Elwell Ferry Rd. (Look for the Trinity United Methodist Church.) Proceed 1.5 miles to the ferry landing.
Total est. distance: 29.5 miles
Total est. time: 45 minutes

Elizabethtown, NC, to Elwell Ferry landing (north/east side of Cape Fear River)

From downtown Elizabethtown proceed north on US 701 N / NC 242 N / NC 41 E for 5.3 miles to intersection with NC 53 at White Lake. Turn right (east) on NC 53 and continue 16.5 miles through the community of Lagoon to the intersection with Elwell Ferry Rd. (Look for the Trinity United Methodist Church.) Turn right (south) on SR 1730 / Elwell Ferry Road. Proceed 1.5 miles to the ferry landing.
Total est. distance: 23.3 miles
Total est. time: 35 minutes

Sans Souci Ferry
SCHEDULE

Map and directions, pp. 178–79

Woodward Rd. to Sans Souci Rd.	
MARCH 16–SEPTEMBER 15	
first crossing 6.30 am	---
Ferry runs on demand throughout the day, seven days a week	
---	last crossing 6.00 pm
SEPTEMBER 16–MARCH 15	
first crossing 7.00 am	---
Ferry runs on demand throughout the day, seven days a week	
---	last crossing 5.00 pm

CHAPTER **16** **Sans Souci Ferry Cashie River**

---

cable-guided vehicle ferry

route Crosses Cashie River, connecting Woodward Rd. and Sans Souci Rd. off NC 308 outside town of **Windsor** (pop. 2,243, Bertie County)

duration 5 min

distance 100 yards

vessels One cable ferry (2 vehicles, 17 passengers)

fare Free

reservations No

schedule
March 16–Sept. 15
6.30 am–6.00 pm daily
Sept. 16–March 15
7.00 am–5.00 pm daily
on demand, weather and water conditions permitting

information
www.albemarle-nc.com/windsor/attractn/sanssouc.htm

shore facilities Ferry office (south side); no public restrooms or other facilities on either side

ON THE MAP OF COASTAL NORTH CAROLINA, *the pinpoint of Sans Souci sits not far from where the long arm of Albemarle Sound crooks its muscular elbow into Bertie County. Here the farmed-and-forested land pours numerous tributaries into the sound, among them the Cashie River, which the ferry crosses near its confluence with the larger Roanoke.*

In the wake of wind and water damage by hurricanes of the past decades, the landscape is eerie with crippled trees, downed timber that forms an impassable-looking jumble over flooded bottomlands. We skirt the swamp on elevated causeways.

The irony isn't lost on us that, coming up from Plymouth, we must cross several rivers by bridge—including the Cashie—in order to reach the ferry crossing for the same river.

Following the winding gravel road off Highway 308 on the north side and coming down a grade, we reach river level and see a nice picnic spot. But no sign of the expected ferry landing. Is this the right place? Our best guess is we're supposed to continue on the dirt road bearing left parallel to the river—but there are some awfully imposing puddles, and as far as we are able to spy ahead, it looks as though the river has overwashed the shallow bank and flooded the road in places.

The **Ferries** of North Carolina   **173**

Eldridge Baker pilots the Sans Souci ferry

We don't know how wise it is to proceed—but going back will mean steering around the low places in reverse, since there's nowhere wide enough to turn around.

Persistence is soon rewarded, though, and we reach land's end. Quite literally.

With some hesitation we tap the horn. In short order we hear an engine crank up, and the boat chugs faithfully toward us like a reluctant but obedient old dog. The current tries to push the ferry downstream, but the operator expertly maneuvers the boat's flat prow onto the only patch of gravel that isn't submerged, stopping a few yards short of our vehicle.

The ferryman—Eldridge Baker of Baker Services, I learn—lowers the ramp, raises the barricade, lets us on, puts the barricade back, raises the ramp, and starts the motor again, punctuating these motions with an occasional chomp on an unlit cigar.

"I thought you might not come for us," I say, thanking him. "We didn't know the water was so high."

Baker gnaws his cigar. "Days like this, most of 'em just come down here and take a look and turn away."

It's all in a day's work for Baker, though, who's seen even four-wheelers get stuck in the muddy marsh and have to be towed out. Baker, who took over the state contract for the ferry route from Britt Services in 2004, says that the river has been unusually high this winter, sometimes causing the ferry to close. But in the busy summer season, a surprising number of tourists as well as locals travel the ferry—maybe twenty a day, forty on the peak July Fourth weekend. Lots of in-staters make the crossing out of curiosity because they've heard something about the little two-car ferry.

It takes only a few minutes to reach the other side, where the riverbank is bordered by stately sweetgum, black gum, and tupelo trees. As we look back where we came from, among the forest we can hardly make out any sign of the landing at all. We've been safely delivered to high ground.

In the cozy ferry house on the other side, a modern structure built on the site of an older one, Baker tells me a bit about his job and the history of the place. With his recliner positioned so he can watch out the window and a gas heater to keep the little shack toasty, he gets a few minutes to sit back and enjoy his cigar. His miniature

Doberman puppy, Cricket, clambers up to keep him company. The dog bounds out the door to hop a ride any time his master needs to take to boat across.

The first time Baker, who grew up in nearby Merry Hill, crossed the ferry years ago, it was a wooden boat with a cable tied to a big cypress tree. Back in those days, the lumbermen in the area were still pulling two-foot-diameter logs out of the swamps, cutting them with an axe.

Some folks around here say the name of the place and its ferry originated in the day when ships would stop here, close to the mouth of the river. One captain wrote on his report "Sans souci," interpreted to mean "not worthwhile."

Local photographer and author Doward Jones, Jr., relates a different legend, in a November 2005 article for Our State magazine. The U.S. postmaster at some point in the 1800s asked the owner of the ferry property what he'd like the new post office at the site to be called. "I don't care," the man replied—and the federal government, though not typically known for its wit, assigned it the French version of the phrase "without a care."

THE TWISTING, SCENIC, 27-MILE **Cashie River** (pronounced CASH-eye) holds the distinction of being the world's longest river contained entirely within the bounds of a single county. According to Doward Jones, there's been a ferry on this site since 1722, when a man by the name of Tomlinson applied to establish one. For nearly three hundred years since, flat-bottomed boats have been poled or pulled across, carrying passengers and cargoes, primarily crops and animals and naval stores.

Finding the signs to the river ferries

High water on the Cashie River

takes a sharp eye. On the south side, cotton fields line the sides of the road to Woodard. Further along on Woodard Road, you'll pass the Cashie United Methodist Church, the Mt. Aire Apostolic Holiness Church, and the St. Paul Baptist Church. Near the ferry landing on the north side, a comfortable-looking community of vacation getaway homes has sprung up.

The rivers and streams and swamps of this watery region are worth exploring. The private organization Roanoke River Partners has established the Roanoke River Paddle Trail along the quiet blackwater courses of the Roanoke and Cashie, along with a network of camping platforms (see www. roanokeriverpartners.org).

For an outdoor experience with a differ-ent—and more spiritual—twist, get in touch with Gail Legett-Robertson at Morningstar Nature Refuge in Williamston, which is free and open to the public by appointment.

•

The hamlet of **Woodard** provides no services for the traveler; the town of **Windsor,** upstream, is the nearest municipality. You'll find a short list of facilities here, from the Windsor Motel to the Inn at Gray's Landing B&B (with its full-service bistro). Check out the Owl Prowl canoeing excursion or other Outdoor Adventure packages. Nearby, circa 1803 Hope Plantation and the Roaoke-Chowan Heritage Center feature heritage exhibits.

Williamston, the largest nearby town, has two campgrounds, four B&Bs, a commu-

The ferry approaches the far bank.

nity college, a convention center, numerous chain motels, and everything from fast food to fine dining.

Across the Roanoke River, **Plymouth** is a waterfront and railroad town with plenty of history, outdoor recreation, and craft to offer. There are several choices for dining and overnight lodging.

If you're interested in reading about the region, pick up a copy of Lucia Peel Powe's novel *Roanoke Rock Muddle* (2003) or thumb through Doward N. Jones, Jr.'s text and images inspired by artist and native son Francis Speight in *Following Francis: A Photographic Journey Through Bertie County* (2005).

For more information
• Windsor Area Chamber of Commerce, 252.794.4277
• Martin County Chamber of Commerce, 252.792.4131
• Martin County Travel and Tourism Office, 1.800.776.8566
• Town of Plymouth (Washington County), 252.793.9101

Exceptionally high river levels force the ferry to suspend service on rare occasion.

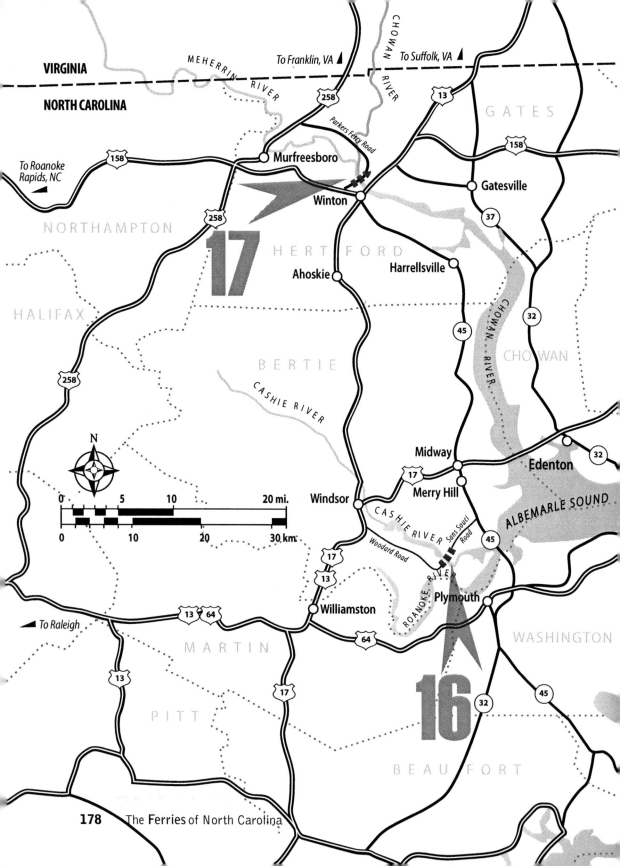

VIRGINIA

NORTH CAROLINA

MEHERRIN RIVER

CHOWAN RIVER

To Franklin, VA ▲

To Suffolk, VA ▲

GATES

258

13

158

Parkers Ferry Road

158

To Roanoke
Rapids, NC
▲

Murfreesboro

Gatesville

NORTHAMPTON

258

Winton

37

17

HERTFORD

Harrellsville

Ahoskie

CHOWAN RIVER

45

32

HALIFAX

BERTIE

CHOWAN

CASHIE RIVER

N

258

Midway

Edenton

32

Merry Hill

17

5   10   20 mi.

ALBEMARLE SOUND

0

Windsor

CASHIE RIVER

Sans Souci Road

45

0   10   20   30 km.

17

Woodard Road

ROANOKE RIVER

13

Plymouth

To Raleigh ▲

13   64

Williamston

64

WASHINGTON

MARTIN

17

16

32

45

13

PITT

BEAUFORT

Sans Souci Ferry GETTING THERE

Plymouth, NC, to Sans Souci ferry landing (east/north bank of Cashie River)

In downtown Plymouth, take US 64 / NC 32 / E. Main St. 1 mile east to the intersection with Mackeys Rd. Turn left onto Mackeys Rd.; proceed 2.2 miles and then turn left (northwest) onto NC 308 / NC 45. Continue 3.9 miles, crossing the bridges over the Roanoke, Middle, and Cashie Rivers. Just past the bridge, at Cashoke Landing, turn left (west) onto NC 308, Cooper Hill Rd. Continue 3.3 miles; around a curve, look for the St. Luke Missionary Baptist Church. Turn left at the church onto SR 1500 / Sans Souci Rd./Woodard Rd. (gravel road). Proceed 1.8 miles to the ferry landing, which will be off to the left at the bottom of the hill past a picnic shelter.
Total est. distance: 12.3 miles
Total est. time: 25 minutes

Windsor, NC, to Sans Souci ferry landing (east/north bank of Cashie River)

From downtown Windsor, take NC 308 / S. King St. south toward Dundee St. Continue to follow NC 308 east for 1.5 miles; turn right to stay on NC 308. Continue east for 8.4 miles; look for the St. Luke Missionary Baptist Church. Turn right at the church onto SR 1500 / Sans Souci Rd./Woodard Rd. (gravel road). Proceed 1.8 miles to the ferry landing, which will be off to the left at the bottom of the hill past a picnic shelter.
Total est. distance: 12 miles
Total est. time: 25 minutes

Edenton, NC, to Sans Souci ferry landing (east/north bank of Cashie River)

From downtown Edenton, take US 17 S for 10 miles, crossing the bridge over the Chowan River. In the community of Midway (Bertie Co.), turn left (south) onto NC 45 S. Proceed 3.6 miles, through community of Merry Hill, then turn right onto SR 1500 / Sans Souci Rd. Continue 6.2 miles (crossing NC 308 at the St. Luke Missionary Baptist Church) to the ferry landing, which will be off to the left at the bottom of the hill past a picnic shelter.
Total est. distance: 20 miles
Total est. time: 35 minutes

Williamston, NC, to Sans Souci ferry landing (west/south bank of Cashie River)

From downtown Williamston, take US 17 N / US 13 N north across the Roanoke River Wetlands toward Windsor. Continue for 9 miles. Turn right (southeast) onto SR 1500 / Woodard Rd.; proceed 10.5 miles on curving road, through the crossroads of Woodard, to the Sans Souci ferry landing.
Total est. distance: 19.5 miles
Total est. time: 35 minutes

Windsor, NC, to Sans Souci ferry landing (west/south bank of Cashie River)

From downtown Windsor, take S. Granville St. 1 mile to the intersection of US 17 S / US 13 S. Proceed 1.5 miles south. Turn left (southeast) onto SR 1500 / Woodard Rd.; proceed 10.5 miles on curving road, through the crossroads of Woodard, to the Sans Souci ferry landing.
Total est. distance: 13 miles
Total est. time: 25 minutes

Beautiful architecture is characteristic of the historic towns of the Albemarle region, such as Williamston, Windsor, Plymouth, Edenton, Ahoskie, and Winton.

Parker's Ferry
SCHEDULE

GETTING THERE
Map, p. 178

Murfreesboro, NC, to Parkers Ferry (south bank of Meherrin River)
From downtown Murfreesboro take US 258 / E. Main St. east for 0.6 miles. At intersection, stay straight to go onto US 158 Bus. Proceed east for 1.5 miles, then turn left onto US 158. Continue 6.9 miles, through the community of Mapleton, to NC 1175 / Parkers Fishery Road / NC 1306 (look for Rivers Correctional Facility on left). Turn left (north) and proceed 3 miles down the gravel road to the ferry landing.
Total est. distance: 12 miles
Total est. time: 20 minutes

Ahoskie, NC, to Parkers Ferry (south bank of Meherrin River)
From downtown Ahoskie, take US 13 N / Academy St. north for 8 miles, bearing right at the community of California, to the intersection with US 158 outside Winton. Turn left (west) on US 158 and proceed 0.9 miles to NC 1175 / Parkers Fishery Road / NC 1306 (look for Rivers Correctional Facility on right). Turn right (north) and proceed 3 miles down the gravel road to the ferry landing.
Total est. distance: 12 miles
Total est. time: 20 minutes

Gatesville, NC, to Parkers Ferry (south bank of Meherrin River)
From downtown Gatesville, take NC 137 west for 8.5 miles through the community of Eure to the intersection with US 13 at Storys. Turn left (southwest) on US 158 and continue 4.1 miles, crossing the Chowan River bridge, to the town of Winton. Turn right (west) on US 158 and proceed 0.9 miles to NC 1175 / Parkers Fishery Road / NC 1306 (look for Rivers Correctional Facility on right). Turn right (north) and proceed 3 miles down

Meherrin River	
MARCH 16–SEPTEMBER 15	
first crossing 6.30 am	---
Ferry runs on demand throughout the day, seven days a week	
---	last crossing 6.00 pm
SEPTEMBER 16–MARCH 15	
first crossing 7.00 am	---
Ferry runs on demand throughout the day, seven days a week	
---	last crossing 5.00 pm

the gravel road to the ferry landing.
Total est. distance: 19 miles
Total est. time: 30 minutes

Murfreesboro, NC, to Parkers Ferry (north bank of Meherrin River)
From downtown Murfreesboro, turn right onto US 258 / US 158 Bus. / E. Main St. Continue to follow US 258 northeast for 5.3 miles, across the Meherrin River and through the community of Barretts Crossroads, to Parkers Ferry Rd. Turn right (southeast) and proceed 4 miles down the gravel road to the ferry landing.
Total est. distance: 9.3 miles
Total est. time: 15 minutes

CHAPTER 17 Parker's Ferry Meherrin River

cable-guided vehicle ferry

route Crosses Meherrin River on Parkers Ferry Rd., off US Hwy. 13/158 outside town of **Winton** (pop. 956, Hertford County)

duration 5 min

distance 75 yards

vessels One cable ferry (2 cars / 17 passengers)

fare Free

reservations No

schedule
March 16–Sept. 15
6.30 am–6.00 pm daily
Sept. 16–March 15
7.00 am–5.00 pm daily
on demand, weather and water conditions permitting

information
Web Though there is no official site for information on Parker's Ferry, updated schedules are generally similar to those for the Sans Souci ferry, which are posted at www.albemarle-nc.com/windsor/attractn/sanssouc.htm

shore facilities Public boat ramps, both sides of river; no public restrooms or other facilities on either side

AFTER A TREK ACROSS THREE COUNTIES IN *in search of this northernmost of the state's river ferries, we follow the dirt road late on this Sunday afternoon, hoping it's the right one. Just past a barricade gravel gives way to riverbank, and a sign provides terse instructions:* Blow Horn for Ferry. *Will it work? Will the magic sound summon the ferryman from the other side to fetch us?*

I press the horn once, like a polite touch on a doorbell, and its raucous noise echoes off the tupelo trees on the far bank. It's so quiet out here on the Meherrin River that the lone sound threatens to drown out Sabbath naps for miles around. But it is answered, after a decent interval, by the cranking of a diesel generator and a churning sound like a trolling motor approaching. A no-nonsense figure in an orange meshback cap patiently maneuvers the craft toward our side of the river. The water is high, but the ferry operator makes it look easy to keep the vessel on its arrow-straight course.

The ferry, which is little more than a small barge with two guardrails, a wheelhouse, and at either end a ramp that raises like a drawbridge, is tethered to a submerged steel cable that spans the river. The boat can't stray far—though it can, in strong currents, get its rudders entangled in the cable. The ferry has two hydraulic propellers to keep it going, in fact; if the cable were to break, props alone aren't strong enough to move it across the current. The operator guides the unassuming craft with practiced skill, cutting the engine at just the right place and time to let the bow drift to rest at the landing.

Passing powerboats slip beneath the cable that guides the ferryboat; the cable must be lowered for larger vessels.

Mary Smith lowers the drawbridge, and I drive the car over the moat and into the castle. Another push of the hydraulic control, and the gate is up again. Smith walks over to the wheelhouse and puts the vessel in motion. Of course the boat faces the same direction on either trip—so it simply slides back along the cable like a pearl on a necklace until she steers it to the opposite landing and reverses the process.

A middle-aged woman steps out of the wheelhouse to meet me. I tell her I wasn't sure we'd arrived in time. Or maybe the river was too high? But now that the boat's on this side, we're obligated to cross: the ferrywoman's own pickup is waiting on the opposite bank, and when she takes us over, that'll be the end of her work day.

Mary Smith is employed by Britt Services, Inc., out of Dunn, N.C., a contracting firm that also handles the Elwell Ferry. (The contractor arrangements have since changed, and Mary Smith retired from ferrying in 2004, after nearly ten years of service.) Mary's husband, Kent, manages the business side of their team, hiring people to work shifts at the ferry. There are two shifts—two people to work each ferry. She gets a week on, then a week off, operating the ferry from dawn to dusk.

As we cross over—a process that takes only about five minutes—I ask what it's like to be a woman out here in the woods, working this lonely and potentially risky job.

"It gets a bit worrisome sometimes," she says laconically, but she doesn't impress me as the sort to ever grow too anxious. And she has lots of company. A busy day might bring 32 vehicles, mostly one at a time; today, in early June, she's ferried 25, including four motorcycles and a truck.

Many of her passengers are locals who work for the prison or the schools, she says. When the ferry is out of commission—as it was for three months last year, when it was pulled out of the water for refurbishing—it takes folks fifteen minutes longer to drive to the nearest bridge crossing. Smith doesn't think it likely the little ferry will be replaced by a bridge—it would require too long an approach, over broad expanses of water and swamp, to provide the height needed to accommodate boating traffic. And besides, there's been a ferry here since

Mary Smith, operator at Parker's Ferry, recently retired from ferrying.

at least the early 1900s. Before the installation of the cable and the steel-decked boat, a wooden barge was hitched to a rope, and even before that, it's likely the early settlers and Indians crossed by raft or boat at this point. Why change things now?

Sure, the river runs high, or the wind kicks up, or a thunderstorm approaches, and you don't want to be caught out in the channel in those conditions.

"There are times myself when I'm scared to cross," Smith admits. The river is 28 to 30 feet deep at this point, a relatively narrow stretch. The perpendicular-crossing ferry can't move out of the way of powerboats coming around the bend, so it's up to the other vessels to keep a sharp eye out. In the fall of 2003 when Hurricane Isabel blew water out of the river, it revealed

the hulk of a boat wrecked here a long time back. Most days, though, it's quiet in the operator's shack, and Smith sees more skunks, bobcats, deer, geese, and turkeys than people.

The sun is setting behind the tall tupelos, and even ferry operators have dinner to get home to. Mary Smith chains up the boat, lowers the barricade, and waves me off, up the gravel road on the far side. I spur the Honda with a bit of gas and roll up the window. Climbing the slight grade away from the riverbank seems like a motion out of long-ago days, a buckboard with a team to do the pulling, the golden light a scene from a vintage film. We pull to a halt where the road joins the highway again, then turn left, westward, back into the twenty-first century again.

Parker's Ferry in the 1920s, when it consisted of a wooden platform guided by a rope (courtesy North Carolina State Archives)

NEAR THE ANCESTRAL MEHERRIN Indian town of Ramushouuong, the Jordan family of Winton, N.C., farmed extensive holdings on both sides of the Meherrin River before the Civil War.

The Jordans established the ferry as a way to transport animals and equipment from one part of their farmland to the other, a practice continued by Pattie Jordan Parker and her husband, Isaac, who attached their name to the ferry in the early 1880s. The Parkers' crossing became popular with north-south travelers, and by 1886 Hertford County commissioned a new ferryboat and soon took over operations. The ferry

remained under county management until 1931, when the State of North Carolina assumed control of highways and ferries.

Black bears have been common in the area, and one long-ago ferrykeeper used to nail bear skins to the sides of barns near the landing. Frank Stephenson, in his book *Parker's Ferry: Hertford County, North Carolina*, recalls that moonshine was a commonly produced commodity in the region as well, often leading to altercations between locals and bounty hunters in earlier decades.

Like the state's other river ferries, these days this one attracts riders as much for enjoyment as for convenience. In 1980, a couple were married on the ferryboat. Movie directors have shot footage for films here; *National Geographic* did a magazine feature in 1979. According to ferry operator William Britt, interviewed for a *Raleigh News & Observer* article in 1977, "People from New York come down to fish and people from other countries have come through. They don't come to see this, 'course, but they love it when they see it."

•

The ferry is situated near the point where the Meherrin River empties into the larger Chowan, which eventually flows into Albemarle Sound. The Virginia state line lies only ten miles to the north, across rolling farmland with no town larger than a crossroads.

On the south bank of the Meherrin River, historic **Winton** is located two and a half miles below the ferry, in one of North Carolina's oldest populated regions. In years past, fishing and other maritime enterprises, as well as a tobacco mill, were linchpins of the economy. Today there are two steel mills nearby, as well as the 1,450-bed low-security Rivers Correctional Facililty; employees from the northern part of the county often use the ferry to save them time getting to work on the Winton side. The Chowan River and its tributaries are popular sites for recreational fishing as well.

The town has a small grocery store, a convenience store, and a couple of restaurants. B&Bs and motels are located in **Murfreesboro** (10 minutes west) and **Ahoskie** (10 minutes south).

Camping is available at the Chowan River Resort in Winton, two miles south of town at Tuscarora Beach.

For more information
• Ahoskie Chamber of Commerce, 252.332.2042

Peaceful waters: Parker's Ferry today is a tranquil and scenic spot.

As long as the sign's not turned to face you when you approach one of the river ferries, you can count on service dawn to dusk, every day of the year.

can't get enough?
further information on **ferries**

This reading list is not meant to be comprehensive; it's a mixed bag of history, technology, picture books, and literature, limited to North America only. Many of the best books are out of print; many local histories are published by small presses and may take some effort to locate. A search on one of the online book merchants for "ferries" and "ferry" will yield dozens of other publications of niche interest besides these.

General reference

Perry, John. *American Ferry Boats*. New York: Wilfred Funk, 1957.

Wright, Sarah Bird. *Ferries of America: A Guide to Adventurous Travel*. Atlanta: Peachtree Publishers, 1987, 1992.

Dod, S. Bayard. *The Evolution of the Ferryboat*. Railroadians of America, 1988.

Bloch, Arnold. *The Physical and Operating Characteristics of Ferry Vessels*. Transportation Training and Research Center, Polytechnic Institute of New York, 1980.

Tupper, E. C. *Ferry Transit Systems for the Twenty First Century*. Society of Naval Arcihtects and Marine Engineers, 2000.

Ferries in North America (east to west)

Murphy, Michael. *Ferryliner Vacations in North America: Ocean Travel and Inland Cruising*. Dutton, 1988. Paperback, 277 pages. ISBN 0525483551. "Ferryliner trips are here distinguished from cruises in that a cruise may be considered a vacation or floating resort in itself while the ferryliner is functional transportation on the water, with basic cabins and meals to sustain the passengers en route. . . . Included here are ferryliners from Alaska to Mexico with data on routes, fares, seasons, vehicle transport, reservations, tickets, and accommodations. Of interest to those who would like to travel economically by ship." — *Library Journal*

Payzant, Joan M., and Lewis J. Payzant. *Like a Weaver's Shuttle: A History of the Halifax-Dartmouth Ferries*. Nimbus Publishers, 1979.

Roberts, Franklin B. *The Boats We Rode: A Quarter Century of New York's Excursion Boats and Ferries*. Quadrant Press, 1974. 100 pages.

Sciascia, Bob. *Ferry Tales: Wit, Wisdom, and a Bartender's Secrets from the Bar of the Port Jefferson Ferry*. BookSurge, 2005.

Olsen, Brian P. *History of Transportation across the Straits of Mackinac*.

Hilton, George Woodman. *Great Lakes Car Ferries: An Endangered Species.*

Mellin, John A. *Ferry Boats (II).* Capital Gazette, 1983.

Oxford, William. T*he Ferry Steamers: The Story of the Detroit-Windsor Ferry Boats.* Boston Mills Press, 1995. 128 pages.

Huntley, James L. *Ferryboats in Idaho.* Caxton Printers Ltd., 1978. Paperback, 279 pages.

Sutter, Annie. *The Old Ferryboats of Sausalito.* Scope Pub. Co., 1987. 35 pages.

Ferries of the South. La Siesta Press, 1964. (California.) 39 pages.

Olmsted, Nancy. *Simple Pleasures Begin with Ferryboats.* San Francisco, Calif.: National Maritime Museum Association, 1999. 52 pages. Ferryboats in San Francisco Bay Area maritime history. www.maritime.org

Delbridge, Joyce. *Northwest Ferry Tales: A Collection of Stories, Poems and Anecdotes from Washington, British Columbia and Alaska.* Vashon Point Productions, 1989.

Faber, Jim. *Ferry Guide: How Best to Use America's Largest Ferry Fleet for Work and Recreation.* (Washington State.) 27 pages.

Kline, Mary Stiles. *Ferryboats: A Legend on Puget Sound.* University of Washington Press, 1983.

Neal, Carolyn, and Thomas Kilday Janus. *Puget Sound Ferries: From Canoe to Catamaran.* American Historical Press, 2001. Hardcover, 220 pages. An illustrated history of the ferries of Puget Sound.

Skalley, Michael. *The Ferry Story: The Evergreen Fleet in Profile.* Superior Pub., 1983. 152 pages.

Stein, Alan J. *Safe Passage: The Birth of Washington State Ferries, 1951–2001.* 2001. Available exclusively from "Ferry Boat Shop Online" at www.ferryboatshop.com/products. "In this book, published to commemorate the 50th anniversary of Washington State Ferries, historian Alan Stein retraces the development of the legendary Black Ball system, the political and personality clashes that led to its undoing, and how state government worked to assure a 'safe passage' for Puget Sound commuters."

Cross, Paul. *Ferry Fare: A Brief History of the Drummond Island Ferries.* Drummond Island Beacon Journal, 1989. 22 pages.

Ommundsen, Peter D. *Bowen Island Passenger Ferries.* Cape West Publishing, 1997. The story of early travel to the Bowen Island holiday resort during the period 1921–1956, with numerous photos of early Canadian ferries. Paperback, 64 pages.

Demar, Robert E., and Robin Atkins. *Nautical Highways: Ferries of the San Juan Islands.* Tiger Press (WA), 2002. Paperback, 72 pp. An art/photography book about the ferry boats of the Pacific Northwest.

O'Malley, Michael F. *Ferry Travel Adventures in Washington, British Columbia and Alaska.* RSH Media, 1996. Paperback: 292 pages.

Ennes, Judith. *Kalakala Comes Home: No Dream Is Too Big!* Puget Sound Press, 2000. A children's story, with original hand-drawn illustrations about Alaska's famous *Kalakala* ferry. Reading level: ages 4–8.

Russell, Steven J. *Kalakala: Magnificent Vision Recaptured.* Puget Sound Press, 2002.

Simpson, Sherry, and Mark Kelley. *Alaska's Ocean Highways: A Travel Adventure Aboard Northern Ferries.* Epicenter Press, 1995.

Ferries in fiction

Gower, Iris. *Fiddler's Ferry.* Severn House Publishers, 2002. 384 pages. ISBN 0727857789. A historical novel set in Wales following World War I. (OK, so we know this isn't North America—but readers might enjoy it anyway.)

Moyes, Patricia. *Night Ferry to Death* (An Inspector Henry Tibbett Mystery). New York: Holt, 1986.

Children's books

Briggs, Martha Wren, and Ella L. Beale. *The Little Ferry's Christmas.* (Travels With Virginia, the Little Ferry, Bk. 1.) Dory Press. Reading level ages 4–8. Wren and Beale have continued their Little Ferry series with several more,

Bald Head Island Ferries captain Joe Miller, seaman Steve Woolson

including *The Little Ferry Meets the Colonial Ships* and *The Little Ferry Goes to the Paper Mill*. Reading levels vary.

Flanagan, Alice K., and Christine Osinski. *Riding the Ferries with Captain Cruz.* (Our Neighborhood, New York, N.Y.) Children's Press, 1997. 32 pages. An illustrated book about riding the Staten Island Ferry.

Maestro, Betsy, and Giulio Maestro. *Ferryboat.* Reading level baby–preschool. "Author Betsy Maestro and artist Giulio often ride the Chester-Hadlyme Ferry near their home in Connecticut. This book is fashioned after that ferry . . . . The author carefully explains the workings of the ferry and takes readers from shore to shore, lovingly describing the sights and sounds of the ride." — *Publishers Weekly*

Rockwell, Anne F. *Ferryboat Ride.* Reading level ages 4–8. "Rockwell and Smith take youngsters on a breezy yet exhilarating anticipatory ride aboard a ferry transporting a girl and her family to their 'summer island.' — *Publishers Weekly*

Schaefer, Lola M. *Ferries.* (Transportation Library.) Bridgestone Books, 2000. Reading level ages 4–8.

Walker, Pamela. *Ferry Rides.* (Welcome Books: Let's Go!) Conn.: Children's Press, 2000. Reading level baby–preschool.

Williamson-Noble, John. *Fergus the Ferry.* Australian children's picture books. From the author: "I wrote the Fergus the Ferry stories while travelling to work on the Rose Bay ferry. I read them to my

Near Small, N.C., on the way to the Aurora ferry

son Tom—he was about 18 months old. Telling Fergus the Ferry stories became something we did on Sundays—while going for a ride on the harbour beaches ferry, which in the summer goes from Watsons Bay to Balmoral to Manly and back to Watsons Bay. We also made some of the stories up while sitting on the back of the ferry—sometimes in rhyming couplets, sometimes in not-so-rhyming couplets."

Young, Ruth, and Marcia Sewall. *Daisy's Taxi*. Orchard Books, 1991.

sources used in this book

Information on place names comes mainly from William S. Powell, *The North Carolina Gazetteer: A Dictionary of Tar Heel Places* (Chapel Hill: University of North Carolina Press, 1968).

Population figures (c. 2006) are taken from **www.epodunk.com** or individual community/county websites. Map directions are adapted from **mapquest.com** and other online mapping services and supplemented with the author's own routes and mileage calculations.

Sarah Bird Wright's *Ferries of America: A Guide to Adventurous Travel* (Atlanta, Ga.: Peachtree Publishers, 1987, 1992) was first published nearly two decades ago by a fellow Southerner. It remains the definitive guide, though equipment has been updated on many of the nation's ferry routes and a number of routes have been changed or added.

John Perry's *American Ferryboats* (New York: Wilfred Funk, 1957), long out of print, is still the only comprehensive history in the field.

On the history of transportation in North Carolina, I consulted Alan D. Watson, *Internal Improvements in Antebellum North Carolina* (Raleigh: Office of Archives and History, 2002). On the background of ferries, I cite information from the *Encyclopedia Americana* (2000 edition) and the online encyclopedia **www.wordiq.com** (s.v. ferry).

Studying what has been written about ferry systems in other parts of the continent was both helpful and fascinating. The ferries of the Pacific Northwest and the Canadian Maritimes always seem to elicit powerful writing, and I learned a great deal from the Web sites of the Washington State Ferries, the Alaska State Ferries, the ferries of the Canadian Maritimes, and the BC (British Columbia) Ferries.

> www.wsdot.wa.gov
> www.bcferries.bc.ca
> www.bayferries.com
> www.peiferry.com

Eldrige Baker and Cricket, Sans Souci Ferry

The newspapers and popular magazines of North Carolina have covered nearly every angle, from the historic to the tourist-oriented, from the economic to the inspirational, related to the state's ferries. Their citations would be too numerous to mention here. But readers doing further research would find the coastal newspapers and periodicals most useful:

Brunswick Beacon (Shallotte, NC) www.brunswickbeaon.com
Daily Advance (Elizabeth City, NC) www.dailyadvance.com
Island Breeze (Hatteras, NC) www.islandbreezepublishing.com
Star-News (Wilmington, NC) www.starnewsonline.com
State Port Pilot (Southport, NC) www.stateportpilot.com
Virginian-Pilot (Hampton Roads, VA) www.hamptonroads.com; www.pilotonline.com often
covers the northeastern North Carolina ferries and other maritime issues.

The statewide periodicals have also done frequent features and provided news coverage on ferry-related issues. Compiled clippings from North Carolina newspapers may be consulted by subject ("ferries," in this case) in the North Carolina Room of the Louis Round Wilson Library, University of North Carolina–Chapel Hill.

News & Observer (Raleigh, NC) www.newsobserver.com

The Observer (Charlotte, NC) www.charlotte.com

Our State magazine (Greensboro, NC), formerly *The State* www.ourstate.com

Historical information on North Carolina's ferries may be found in

North Carolina Department of Archives and History

North Carolina Room, Wilson Library, University of North Carolina–Chapel Hill

Local histories are invaluable in gleaning details, especially about the small river ferries.

Elwell Ferry, Kelly, North Carolina. Centennial edition. Ed. J. A. McKoy and C. A. Carter. ([Kelly, N.C.]: Kelly Historical Society, 2005).

E. Frank Stephenson, Jr., *Parker's Ferry, Hertford County, North Carolina* ([Murfreesboro, N.C.]: Meherrin River Press, 1996).

On the ferries serving Bald Head Island, and the history of the island, see their website at www.baldheadisland.com. Also about Bald Head Island, see David Stick, *Bald Head: A History of Smith Island and Cape Fear* (Wendell, NC: Broadfoot Publishing, 1985).

Tourist guides in all the coastal communities provide up-to-date information along with a bit of history and interest. There are many book-length travel guides to North Carolina, but the ones I consulted here are:

Glenn Morris, *North Carolina Beaches: A Visit to National Seashores, State Parks, Ferries, Public Beaches, Wildlife Refuges, Lighthouses, Boat Ramps and Docks, Museums, and More*, 3rd. ed. (Chapel Hill: University of North Carolina Press, 2005).

Sara Pitzer, *North Carolina off the Beaten Path*, 7th ed. (Guilford, CT: Globe Pequot Press, 2004). From the useful Insiders' Guides series.

Claiborne S. Young, *Cruising Guide to Coastal North Carolina*, 6th ed. (Winston-Salem: John F. Blair, 2005).

The **North Carolina State Tourism** website, www.visitnc.com, provided basic information as a starting point for my firsthand research.

A great deal of detail about the North Carolina state ferries came from documents and public information from the North Carolina Ferry Division, including a 2004 PowerPoint, "The North Carolina Ferry System," presented by then director Jerry Gaskill, and the Ferry Division's Web site at www.ncferry.org. I found the Ferry Division's unpublished history, based on research of staff member Joe Owens, invaluable.

State of North Carolina, Department of Highways
Ferry Division
113 Arendell St., Morehead City, NC 28557

The **Passenger Vessel Association (PVA)**, www.passengervessel.com, is a trade organization focused on issues and concerns relevant to owners and operators of passenger vessels, car and passenger ferries, eco-tour operators, sightseeing and excursion boats, cruise ships, manufacturers of maritime-related products and services, and other related service companies. It is an excellent source of information on legislation and operation of passenger vessels of all types.